Police Corruption in the NYPD

From Knapp to Mollen

Police Corruption in the NYPD

From Knapp to Mollen

Steven V. Gilbert
University of Phoenix
Phoenix, Arizona, USA

Barbara A. Gilbert
Excelsior College
Albany, New York, USA

CRC Press
Taylor & Francis Group
Boca Raton London New York

CRC Press is an imprint of the
Taylor & Francis Group, an **informa** business

CRC Press
Taylor & Francis Group
6000 Broken Sound Parkway NW, Suite 300
Boca Raton, FL 33487-2742

First issued in hardback 2017

ISBN 13: 978-1-138-41561-4 (hbk)
ISBN 13: 978-1-4987-2153-0 (pbk)

Visit the Taylor & Francis Web site at
http://www.taylorandfrancis.com

and the CRC Press Web site at
http://www.crcpress.com

Contents

Preface

For as long as policing has existed, there have been ongoing acts of corruption. Police officers are granted a status of power, which in many cases has been abused for personal gain. Police corruption is a social phenomenon witnessed every day by the members of the community. More recently, police corruption has gained notoriety with the advent of mobile video cameras in cell phones or through the use of other recording media. Consider the question: Is our society becoming desensitized to acts of corruption of varying severity? Since corruption is so widespread in our society, one particular police agency was selected for examination. Within a 22-year period, the New York Police Department was twice placed under the lens of investigation for systemic corruption. It is unknown to what extent corruption existed within the New York Police Department or how deeply it lives within the department today. Famous corruption cases involving police officers Frank Serpico and Michael Dowd brought corruption to the attention of the public and city administration, prompting Mayor John Lindsay to order the formation of the Knapp Commission and subsequent investigations. Between May 1970 and December 1972, the Knapp Commission was successful in identifying deep systemic corruption. The Knapp Commission concluded that not only did the police officers delve into corruption, but the department administration turned a blind eye to the problem while placing the blame upon the "rogue officer" who was the "bad apple" ruining the department. Even after recommending corrective actions, the New York Police Department was once again investigated for corruption, and this time the corruption was worse. On July 24, 1992, Mayor David Dinkins appointed the Mollen Commission to investigate corruption similar to that of the Knapp Commission investigation. As a result of the 22-month investigation, Mollen reported, "Despite our overall cause for optimism, we found that police corruption is a serious problem confronting our city."

Authors

Dr. Steven V. Gilbert is a retired special agent with the United States Army Criminal Investigation Command. During his tenure with the Army CID, Dr. Gilbert was responsible for investigating a wide variety of felony offenses of which the U.S. government was a party of interest. He has taught criminal justice and forensic sciences since 1987. Among this coursework was curriculum development of the ethics of criminal justice and in interrogations. Dr. Gilbert published his textbook *Interviewing and Interrogation: The Discovery of Truth* in 2004. He earned his doctor of philosophy in criminal justice in 2005. Dr. Gilbert is a professor of forensic science and psychological profiling at the University of Phoenix.

Dr. Barbara A. Gilbert is a forensic nurse educator, teaching courses in legal and ethical issues, criminal justice, education, and nursing. As a nurse educator, Dr. Gilbert has provided instruction for courses in both ground and online classroom environments at the associate, baccalaureate, and master's levels. Her doctoral dissertation was published in 2010, when she earned her doctor of education with a specialization in curriculum and instruction. Dr. Gilbert is a professor of nursing at Excelsior College and the State University of New York Colleges.

1
The Need for External Oversight

> The mission of the New York City Police Department is to enhance the quality of life in our City by working in partnership with the community and accordance with constitutional rights to enforce the laws, preserve the peace, reduce fear, and provide a safe environment.
>
> **NYPD: New York's Finest (2015, para. 1)**

The New York Police Department, which has maintained an approximate population of 31,000 police officers, is a very large agency and provides a wide array of services to the citizens of New York City. These services provide uniformed patrols, detective services, transportation enforcement (transit authority police), organized crime investigation, and housing enforcement. Aside from these standard activities, the department also provides internal investigations such as the Internal Affairs units. These units investigate complaints of acts of corruption and misconduct lodged against officers. The infrastructure of the department has also remained static over the years. For example, the Patrol Services Bureau, which is the largest element of the department, has maintained approximately 30,000 officers. About 20,000 of these officers were assigned to patrol activities. Four hundred and fifty patrolmen and higher ranking officers were assigned as *plain clothes* officers. Finally, 3,000 officers were assigned as detectives. Other personnel worked in various other sections of the department.

On April 25, 1970, *The New York Times* reported that the New York Police Department was experiencing large-scale corruption and that part of the problem was the failure of the police administration to stop it. Not all officers were actively involved in acts of corruption; however, it was found that many officers had passive involvement. The corruptive acts were so blatant that citizens and business owners were witnessing them on a daily basis. Burnham (1970) of *The New York Times* set the tone for the ensuing investigations by titling his article, "Graft Payments to Policemen Here Are Reported to Run Into the Millions; Annually Some Members of Force Say Officials Fail to Act" (p. 1). This exposure prompted then mayor John V. Lindsay to initiate a systemic investigation that would ultimately uncover corruption on a major scale within the police department. Mayor Lindsay's mandate for the investigation outlined four goals: to determine the extent to which corruption existed; to review the current policies and procedures used to investigate claims of corruption and whether these procedures benefitted the citizens of New York City; to make recommendations to improve these procedures; and finally to collect evidence of corruption and to assist in public hearings (Knapp, Monserrat, Sprizzo, Thomas, & Vance, 1972, p. 269). The order to conduct this investigation was provided to the Knapp Commission on May 21, 1970, in Executive Order 11. The commission was provided with the authority to interview police officers, administrators, and citizens by using all means necessary, which included undercover police work and the use of informants. It is important to recall that Officer Frank Serpico, a plainclothes officer, attempted to combat corruption when he was confronted with payoffs from local business owners through his peers. Later in the investigation Mayor Lindsay wrote to Whitman Knapp in which he referred to the Officer Serpico case by stating, "We have come a long way since the Officer Serpico case in 1967 raised allegations of corruption which began the process which culminated in my appointment of your commission" (as cited in Knapp et al., 1972, n.p.). It is interesting to note that 3 years transpired between the Officer Serpico case and the seminal article written by Burnham in 1970. Why did the Knapp Commission investigation require a 3-year hiatus after the Officer Serpico hearings before beginning its investigation?

The Need for Social Change

Once corruption was exposed within the New York Police Department in 1970, it was apparent that social change was needed. Those aware of the department's history were knowledgeable about past corruption scandals. Upon the establishment of the department in 1845 a dichotomy existed which demonstrated that two entities were the driving forces for misconduct and corruption. Unscrupulous citizens preyed upon police officers to suit their needs whether personal or professional. Police officers who were driven by personal gain preyed upon citizens whether they were willingly involved in corruption or not. Aside from these two entities, many seemingly incorruptible officers provided passive assistance. Finally, the police leadership which is responsible for the officers' actions also provided passive assistance by not taking necessary action. Historically, social change existed from the beginning of law enforcement efforts in New York City. The only "change" that made a difference in corruption was the degree to which officers were engaging in acts of misconduct or criminal behaviors. This system of corruption can be likened to that of a social system within the city. By virtue of existence, society itself is a social system. This general description portrays the many individual systems found within society. In the case of the New York Police Department, the culture of corruption became its own social system with its unique members. The question is how did this social system become strengthened to the degree that a major investigation was warranted? To understand this phenomenon, one has to examine how these systems develop.

During the Knapp and Mollen eras, it was found that corruption and misconduct constituted its own social system. As with any such system, there are subsystems like cultural societies, organizations, governments, and the individual members. Treated as its own system, corruption was supported by its subsystems, namely organized groups of corrupt police officers and citizens, cultural groups as in the narcotics trade, the political administration within the department, and the individual police officer. In the words of the famed cultural anthropologist, Margaret Mead (1999), change is inevitable and it is here to stay.

Ideally, new police officers entered the department with a sense of virtue and the desire to enforce the law and combat crime. Once a person enters a new social system, he or she must undergo efforts to assimilate into that culture and learn how to coexist with other members. Socially, the new officer becomes conditioned to his or her new environment and will change based upon what he or she experiences. Depending upon the goal of the new conditioning, the system can be either supportive or destructive. The conditioning can also occur in two directions; the system can socially condition the officer or the officer can socially condition the system. Participating in systemic corruption and misconduct can be personally and professionally detrimental to an officer. Mead (1999) saw conditioning as a matter of social survival. In her view, people begin their lives mindlessly and need to become conditioned as a matter of defense. In the end, as the members create their own social system, the reverse is found to be true. This will result in the system developing its own laws and principles for the members to follow. The well-known example from law enforcement is that "cops don't rat on cops."

Understanding the complexity of social systems is an important step in envisioning the manner in which corruption and misconduct strengthened in the New York Police Department. There is no evidence indicating the origin of the systemic corruption in the department; was it from the patrol officer to the administration or reverse? Regardless of the direction in which the corruption evolved, one vision was clear; social change was to be an imminent effort on the part of the system upon itself with the assistance of needed external review and oversight.

Challenges to the Department's Social Change

As important as this investigation was, it began with various operational challenges. It is obvious that this type of investigation would require funding. However, due to budgetary constraints the city was only able to provide financial support until December 31, 1970 (Knapp et al., 1972). Not only did the city's limited ability to fund the investigation adversely affect the commission's existence, not all members of the city council were in favor of this action. It was expected that the dissenting council members would be against providing continued financial support. As a result, the commission was able to gain support from the Law Enforcement Assistance Administration (LEAA) for a funding period of 6 months. The total investigative period for the commission was 9 months.

Another challenge was the inability to subpoena testimony and records for future hearings. Again this was contingent upon the funding ability and support of the city council or continued funding from LEAA. At the end of the LEAA funding period, the commission realized a devastating blow to its efforts. Not only did the funding run out without renewal, but the commission staff of 30 members was cut to 6 members which included investigators and attorneys. Subpoena power was also lost when the budget was not renewed. The ultimate loss of funding and subpoena power also resulted in the noncompletion of important investigations. Private sources could not be used since it would entail revealing sensitive information. The investigation then relied upon a small amount of unrestricted funds along with a small grant from the LEAA.

In general, other challenges have existed regarding the investigation of corruption which can be found within the theoretical realm. Quite frequently officers commit acts of corruption, from minor gratuities to felony offenses. In most of these instances, the police department conducts internal investigations to determine if the alleged infractions were founded. There is an interesting dichotomy present when discussing police corruption. Examination of the Knapp report shows that rather small acts of corruption were investigated by the commission. Today, 42 years later, similar acts are relatively ignored by the public or business owners. Is it possible that we as communities have become desensitized regarding corruption? If police officers today continue to receive gratuities, for example, why do the police administrators condone or ignore these acts? In an effort to settle this issue, Kania (2003) offered his views about police corruption in that gratuities are ethical under particular circumstances. When police officers receive gratuities, many believe that a consideration or expectation is established between the citizen and the officer. Does that gratuity result in not being cited for traffic or other infractions? According to Kania (2003) gratuities are ethical if no strings are attached. Kania (2003) also put forth arguments as to why gratuities are acceptable. For instance, a wide variety of professionals are permitted to accept gratuities during their daily practices. Separating the police from these other professionals, how many of these professionals affect the lives of the public as the police officer does? Next, there is nothing wrong with certain people paying more for law enforcement support. Certain businesses may be located in troubled areas and the presence of the police may tend to decrease the chances of robbery or other crimes. This is a consideration since most police departments do not have sufficient personnel to provide frequent protection services. There are ethicists who believe that gratuities can have serious side effects upon the community and condemn their presence in law enforcement.

Aside from receiving such gratuities as free meals it could be argued that a large number of officers were not engaging in corruption. But the question remained: Did the failure of officers to report corruption make them corrupt as well? It is well known that there exists a code of silence among officers. How high does this silence extend? Sööt (2012) found implications where management was a causal factor in the failure to prevent corruption. Once these shortcomings are identified, then remedial education would be warranted. Knapp et al. (1972) also found the New York Police Department administration dismissive in regards to corruption within the department. As a result, officers could learn from management that the appropriate answer to the corruption dilemma was to deny it extended deeply into the organization. Knapp et al. (1972) likened the dismissal of corruption within the department as a means to avoid tension and anxiety. Punch (2010) supported this finding in that corruption does not exist upon individualism but rather collective conspiracies that result in harm to multiple victims. It is important to define "harm" within corruption. Corruption can take several forms; gratuities, on-duty substance abuse, graft, sexual misconduct, and various criminal offenses as will be seen during this discussion (Pollock, 2013). Barker listed other types of corruption as kickbacks, opportunistic thefts, shakedowns, protection of illegal activities, and fixing tickets (as cited in Pollock, 2013). However it must be proved that such acts were intended to result in a consideration or expectation that a service would be provided. This would require interpreting the motives of both the provider of corruption as well as the receiver. Police officers also possess special traits that enable them to perform their duties. Law provides that officers possess the authority to enforce laws. It can exist with or without the powers to demand results. Power, on the other hand, is the ability to force or persuade others to perform certain actions. This can be accomplished through punishment or reward. Power can exist with or without authority. It is clear that power can be abused since it can be used to accomplish criminal intent such as extortion. The commission investigation consisted of 183 witnesses from various walks of life, from city officials to known criminals. Of the witnesses called to testify, 113 were police officers under subpoena, and 68 civilians were subpoenaed.

The Community Involvement in Corruption

What part does the community play in police corruption? Considering officer misconduct, such acts on the part of the officer may occur through physical aggressiveness, nonfeasance, malfeasance, or corruption. Leadership within the police department is responsible for preventing corruptive acts within the ranks. The responsibility for corruption can easily be placed on the environment, which is supported by the failure of leadership. Many officers can engage in acts of force due to their relationship with the public. Inadequate training by leadership can often times fail to prevent personal injury and damage to property. Warren (2011), based upon a study of police and citizen relationships, stated that "Vicarious experiences are therefore important, because the negative accounts of police behavior that are shared in social networks can create a larger culture of distrust that will reduce police trustworthiness among citizens" (p. 357). While officers are trained to accept and disregard verbal abuse, there clearly comes a point where this may reach unacceptable levels. An excellent example of this is the social unrest and looting that occurred in Ferguson, MO. The citizenry, responding to the shooting of Michael Brown by a police officer, confronted the police during violent protests, which resulted in the use of force by the local and state authorities. Eventually, the police permitted protesters to break into stores and steal property in an effort to prevent physical conflict. The potential for corruptive police actions is present in such events. Albeit in the interest of community peacefulness, the omission to prevent such behaviors, in theory, implicates the officers as well. Recall that Sööt (2012) placed responsibility upon the police management which failed to prevent corruption. Knapp et al. (1972) found that the senior management of the police department denied any knowledge or responsibility in regards to corruption and passed the blame onto the *rogue officers* who were regarded as the *bad apples.*

During the Knapp Commission investigation it was recommended that incentives be provided to officers who did their jobs well. Consideration must be taken regarding the environment where officers are in possession of large quantities of money or drugs versus their remuneration. There have been many cases where officers have indulged in drug sales to gain extra income. Table 1.1 documents the pay rate for New York Police Department officers for the fiscal year 1960–1961.

Table 1.1 New York Police Department Uniformed Force Budget for 1960–1961

QUOTA AND SALARIES
CODE 056-19-050

LINE NO. RANK	QUOTA	SALARY ($)
1. Chief Inspector	1	20,124
2. Chief of Detectives	1	13,664
3. Assistant Chief Inspector and Chief of Staff	1	13,664
4. Supervising Assistant Chief Inspector	1	13,664
5. Assistant Chief Inspector	14	11,948
6. Deputy Chief Inspector	20	11,376
7. Inspector	35	10,806
8. Deputy Inspector	55	10,177
9. Commanding Officer, Detective Bureau	1	10,806
10. Assistant Superintendent of Telegraph	1	10,177
11. Captain	238	9,030–9,610
12. Chief Surgeon	1	11,434
13. Deputy Chief Surgeon	1	10,177
14. Surgeon	25	9,031–611
14a. Lieutenant (detailed as Director of Legal Bureau)	1	9,146
15. Lieutenant (Special Assignment)	15	8,106–8,395
16. Lieutenant (Commander, Detective Squad)	47	8,106–8,395
17. Lieutenant	875	7,505–7,794
18. Sergeant (detailed as Supervisor of Detective Squad)	107	7,505–7,794
19. Sergeant (detailed as Special Assignment)	21	7,505–7,794
20. Sergeant	1,498	6,692–6,981
21. Patrolman (detailed as First Grade Detective)	269	7,505–7,794
22. Patrolman (detailed as Second Grade Detective)	450	6,692–6,981
23. Patrolman (detailed as Third Grade Detective)	1,762	6,324
24. Patrolman (detailed as Special Assignment)	67	6,379

(Continued)

Table 1.1 (*Continued*) New York Police Department Uniformed Force Budget for 1960–1961

QUOTA AND SALARIES CODE 056-19-050 LINE NO.		RANK	QUOTA	SALARY ($)
25. Patrolman	9 months	4th Probation Grade		4,761
	3 months	4th Grade		4,761
	1 year	3rd Grade}	18,830	4,961
	1 year	2nd Grade		5,461
	After 3 years	1st Grade		6,076
26. Policewoman (assigned as Director, Bureau of Policewomen)			1	10,177
27. Policewoman (detailed as First Grade Detective)			4	7,505–7,794
28. Policewoman (detailed as Second Grade Detective)			10	6,692–6,981
29. Policewoman (detailed as Third Grade Detective)			35	6,324
30. Policewoman (Grades and Salaries same as Patrolman)			203	
	Total		24,590	

Source: Courtesy of New York City Police Department, New York City, NY.

Even considering the cost of living during the fiscal year of 1960, officers were still exposed to the opportunities to gain more income through corrupt activities. The overall effect upon the community can be devastating even though citizens who partake in police corruption do so voluntarily. Caiden (2013) described corruption from officials such as police officers and administrators as "…wrongful conduct appertaining to transgressions of deeply held norms, beliefs, and ideals that emotionally offend anything that goes astray from commonly held expectations" (p. 93). During the Knapp Commission investigation, many acts of corruption occurred between two consenting parties; the officer and the citizen gaining an expected consideration or favor in return for gratuities and payments to the officer.

More Internal Oversight

Another need for internal oversight is the nature of police departments in general. For example, police departments survive upon the need for loyalty to the group. If the group loyalty is anticorruption, then the fight against corruption may succeed. However, if the group loyalty is pro-corruption, then this fight may fail. Recall that Officer Serpico was involved in anticorruption, which resulted in his ostracization from the group. Officer Serpico and others who combated corruption experienced both suspicion and hostility from the department due to their interference in the nefarious operations. Officers, for the most part, desire to be proud of their organizations. Officers who do not partake in police corruption also tend to feel hostility toward those who cause disruption to the system, namely reporting other officers who are corrupt. This mixture of hostility and pride can result in denials that systemic corruption exists within their departments (Knapp et al., 1972). The famous *rotten apple theory* evolved from a protective stance by the New York Police Department to protect the department's image and morale. In order to be successful in this, all members of the department must reject the idea that systemic corruption exists even though it was an obvious issue.

The police department is primarily responsible for conducting all investigations or inquiries into corruption complaints. Internal oversights, if conducted correctly, can collect evidence of such behaviors and result in resolutions such as prosecutions or dismissals. The alternate approach to corruption by the New York Police Department was found to be true by the Knapp Commission. Various deficiencies were found which prevented the department from investigating corruption. These deficiencies included the lack of authority or manpower to conduct investigations, disorganization of records and investigative procedures, or improper attitudes about conducting the investigations (hostility) (Knapp et al., 1972).

Lamboo (2010) described four aspects of the internal investigations conducted regarding acts of misconduct. These aspects are external oversight, internal or external investigations, relevant procedures, and reactivity and proactivity. There are two methods that can be used to conduct these investigations. The investigation can be an internal inquiry or a review by an independent entity to preclude biased results. The procedures can entail formal, informal, or managerial reviews of the complaint. In an effort to further investigate acts of misconduct, a Civilian Complaint Review Board (CCRB) was instituted in 1993.

The review board is an all-civilian entity chartered with supporting members of the community in their complaints of police misconduct, whether it be corruption or other types of misconduct. There are four main areas in which the review board conducts an unbiased investigation against police officers. These areas are acts of undue force, abuse of authority, discourtesy, and offensive language. Although discourtesy and offensive language are not acts of corruption, undue force and abuse of authority can be. The review board provides civilians with the opportunity to file a complaint either by phone or online (CCRB, 2014).

The Mollen Investigation

On July 7, 1994, Milton Mollen and his commissioners wrote their report aptly referred to as "Anatomy of Failure: A Path for Success." Twenty-two years after Whitman Knapp published his report, the New York Police Department was once again under the lens of investigation for corruption and lack of ethics and integrity. The new Mollen Commission consisted of 5 commissioners, 6 commission counsel, 13 commission investigators, and other staff members. On July 24, 1992, Mayor David N. Dinkins, issued executive order no. 42 wherein he justified the order citing the following:

> WHEREAS, allegations of corruption have been made against some members of the Police Department, and the effectiveness of the practices, procedures and methods used by the police department to prevent and detect misconduct and to maintain integrity has been questioned; and
>
> WHEREAS, an investigation by the Police Department of those allegations would be subject to question by the public; and
>
> WHEREAS, the misdeeds of a few must not be allowed to sully or taint the reputations and sacrifices of the vast majority of honest and dedicated men and women who serve on the police force;
>
> NOW, THEREFORE, by the power vested in me as mayor of the City of New York, it is hereby ordered:...
>
> **As cited in Mollen, Baer, Evans, Lankler, and Tyler (1994, n.p.)**

As seen during the Knapp Commission investigation, Dinkins questioned the wisdom of permitting the New York Police Department to investigate itself. A comparison of Knapp to Mollen will show that the more recent acts of corruption and crimes committed by police officers far surpassed the previous behaviors. Whereas police officers in Knapp received bribes, police officers in Mollen were criminals of serious crimes. Additionally, the leadership of the department was called into the question as well. Was Knapp successful in combating corruption, or was it a temporary recognition of a problem that continued to fester?

References

Burnham, D. (1970, April 25). Graft payments to policemen here are reported to run into the millions annually: Some members of force say officials fail to act. *The New York Times*. Retrieved from: http://query.nytimes.com/gst/abstract.html?res=9E02E5DE1E31E236A05756C2A9629C946190D6CF

Caiden, G. A. (2013). Checkered history of combatting official corruption. *Asian Education and Development Studies, 2*(2), 92–111.

Kania, R. (2003). The ethical acceptability of gratuities: Still saying "Yes" after all these years. *Criminal Justice Ethics, 23*(1), 54–63.

Knapp, W., Monserrat, J., Sprizzo, J., Thomas, F., & Vance, C. (1972). *The Knapp Commission report on police corruption*. New York, NY: Braziller.

Lamboo, T. (2010). Police misconduct: Accountability of internal investigations. *International Journal of Public Sector Management, 23*(7), 613–631. doi: 10.1108/09513551011078888

Mead, M. (1999). *Continuities in cultural evolution*. New Brunswick, NJ: Transaction Publishers.

Mollen, M., Baer, H., Evans, H., Lankler, R., & Tyler, H. R. (1994). *Commission to investigate allegations of police corruption and the anti-corruption procedures of the police department: Commission report*. New York, NY: The City of New York.

New York City Civilian Complaint Review Board. (2014). Welcome to the Civilian Complaint Review Board. Retrieved from: http://www.nyc.gov/html/ccrb/html/home/home.shtml

NYPD: New York's Finest. (2015). *Mission*. Retrieved from: http://www.nyc.gov/html/nypd/html/administration/mission.shtml

Pollock, J. (2013). *Ethical dilemmas and decisions in criminal justice*. Belmont, CA: Wadsworth.

Punch, M. (2010). Police corruption: Apples, barrels and orchards. *Criminal Justice Matters, 79*(1), 10–12. doi: 10.1080/09627250903569890

Sööt, M.-L. (2012). The role of management in tackling corruption. *Baltic Journal of Management, 7*(3), 287–301.

Warren, P. Y. (2011). Perceptions of police disrespect during vehicle stops: A race based analysis. *Crime & Criminology, 57*(3), 356–376.

2
The Knapp Commission Investigation

The reality is that we do not wash our own laundry – it just gets dirtier.

Detective Frank Serpico

A summary was prepared following the commission's investigation. The opening sentence of the summary bluntly pointed out the major finding, "We found corruption to be widespread" (Knapp, Monserrat, Sprizzo, Thomas, & Vance et al., 1972, Summary, para. 1). It was expected that this widespread corruption would include various serious crimes. Knapp et al. (1972) found that the most sophisticated instance of corruption was committed by officers who were responsible for enforcing gambling prohibitions. Further, rather than individual officers receiving gratuities or payments, there was a "...striking standardized pattern of corruption" (Knapp et al., 1972, n.p.) in which plainclothes officers would collect payoffs from gamblers on a biweekly or monthly basis (known as a "pad"). After all collections occurred, the total amount collected was evenly distributed among the officers, which could yield them between $300 and $1,500 (known as the "nut"). Other incidents of corruption were occurring within the city that compelled the need for the Knapp Commission's investigation.

It is important to understand how the Knapp Commission investigation began. Inasmuch as there were complaints from within the department (Officer Serpico, for example), other sources were supplying complaints as well. Many complaints were received from the citizens of New York City, especially from those who resided in the lower socioeconomic areas, or as many from the community described them as slums or ghettos. This is understandable since these citizens were financially deficient and unable to sustain the demands for money or services by unscrupulous police officers. However many, if not most of the complaints were either unsubstantiated or false. The remainders of these complaints were held to be believable due to the repeated substance of the reported incidents. For example, offering to provide protection to business owners was a common theme for the commission investigators and therefore was listed as a potentially truthful complaint. The complaints investigated by the commission arrived in three basic fashions: letters, phone calls, and interviews. At the conclusion of the commission investigation, more than 1,700 written or telephonic complaints were received for investigation (Knapp et al., 1972). Commissioner Robert Rankin, not a member of the Knapp Commission, formed a separate commission to investigate allegations of corruption, which resulted in the arrest of police officers. Rankin supplied the Knapp Commission with 375 complaints for investigation.

"A Somewhat Fatalistic Belief..."

Aside from investigating the various written or verbal complaints from the citizenry, the commission also desired to receive information from those who possessed either experience in corruption or other types of knowledge. In a situation like this, hearsay information could be very dangerous to the outcome of the investigation. Hearsay is defined as a statement made out of court pertaining to a person who is not testifying (Garner, 2014). Absent witnesses cannot be confronted in court therefore their information cannot be examined. Exceptions to hearsay do exist; for example, business records are a common exception and can be admitted as evidence if they are maintained in the normal course of business. Therefore, those making complaints against others or "citing" others could ultimately cause serious damage not only to the results of the investigation but also to the person being accused. The sources identified for the investigation consisted of businessmen, former and present police officers, people involved in criminal behaviors, and those residing in high crime areas of the city. Each type of source was in the position to become involved in acts of corruption with police officers or victimized. Based upon these and other interviews, the commission found that the ordinary New York City citizen had a fatalistic view of the police department, believing the corruption had permeated the department to serious levels (Knapp et al., 1972).

Not surprising was the reaction of the witnesses. Although offered confidentiality, many citizens providing information refused to testify or have their information used in the investigation. This could have indicated that the sources were possibly providing false information and feared that their testimony would result in legal actions against them. Most of the interviews did contain information that supported the belief that the New York Police Department was rife with corruption based upon personal observations of such activities. These refusals to reveal their identities came from police officers as well, even if granted anonymity. At the end of the preliminary investigation, sufficient information was collected to provide the commission with "… a pretty clear picture …" of corruption occurring in the city (Knapp et al., 1972, p. 43). This "pretty clear picture" would later summarize the findings of the commission investigation. The preliminary information collected by the commission indicated that most corruption issues are centered upon the receipt of bribes or payoffs. Repetitiveness was the key to initiating investigations in order to ward off false and misleading information from unreliable sources. The question of why so many people were against the police department while choosing to make false allegations needs to be addressed. It wasn't for the lack of community relations. The New York Police Department operated the Police Athletic League (PAL) for children and teenagers where police officers would foster bonds with children in an effort to steer them away from crime and to develop a sense of trust with the police. In fact, 2014 was the 100th year for the New York PAL program. The PAL was founded by Captain John Sweeney from an East side precinct. The history of PAL is quite extensive and too lengthy to discuss here. Suffice it to say, that between 1914 and 1929, *playstreets* were instituted by Police Commissioner Arthur Woods, an advocate for the poor in the city (Police Athletic League, 2014). The idea of playstreets was to find safe locations for children living in tenements to play; for example, refurbished empty lots or closing residential blocks for short periods of time. Apparently, the Police Athletic League did little to discourage the poor image the police department had in the eyes of the citizenry. Could this fatalistic view of the police come from the social unrest from the 1950s to 1960s? Coupled with the social unrest in the United States and the Vietnam era, police corruption throughout the city continued to grow.

Investigative Techniques

The commission investigators used a variety of standard investigative techniques when addressing suspected incidents of corruption. These techniques included both overt and covert activities. Most of the techniques required covert activities. For example, surveillances were conducted of public areas where possible corruption occurred. These acts of corruption would involve open violations such as illegal parking or other behaviors done in public. Informants were used from both the police force itself, the community, and even from the underworld where identified and arrested offenders would provide information in return for leniency during prosecution. Surreptitious interviews were also recorded through the use of electronic recording instruments commonly known as *wires*. In addition to these techniques, the investigators would also pose as customers for corruption or as law violators so that they would be trusted to engage in acts of corruption. One issue adversely affecting the surreptitious recording of conversations was the legal position of the courts, which held that one party to the conversation must consent to the eavesdropping or recording. Further, the person using this surveillance technique was restricted to the status of a police officer working under the auspices of a search warrant; this prevented nonofficers on the commission from using electronic devices. Initially, the commission lacked the ability to compel officers to testify through subpoena power. Subsequent legal actions were decided in favor of the commission permitting the issuance of subpoenas.

The status of the commission investigator was a benefit for the commission. The investigators had federal law enforcement backgrounds and were not specifically collecting information for criminal purposes. Their status was found to ease witnesses into interviews since they had no official association with the New York Police Department. Considering this, it was apparent that the New York Police Department was unable to police itself. This attitude was a recurring theme throughout the investigation.

The Department's Pyramid of Corruption

At the time of the Knapp investigation, the New York Police Department had approximately 33,450 personnel assigned as law enforcement officers working investigations or patrolling the city

Table 2.1 Strength of the New York Police Department

Commissioner's Office	8
Detective's Bureau	3,000
Plainclothes	450
Patrol Force	30,000
Total Law Enforcement Personnel	33,458

Note: 1972 NYPD law enforcement personnel.

(Knapp et al., 1972), (Table 2.1), as compared to the 2014 total employees of 34,500 employees (NYPD New York's Finest, 2015).

Corruption had existed within the New York Police Department since its inception in 1845. From the beginning, extortion and other types of corruption were found to exist. The city now had an official police department, but the public expressed their shock and displeasure that the officers would extort citizens and indulge in corruptive behaviors for their personal gain. By 1894, the New York Senate ordered an investigation into the department's corruption wherein it was found that systemic extortion existed, mostly within the gambling operations throughout the city (Knapp et al., 1972). This first investigation was conducted by the Lexow Committee funded by private sources; New York State refused to fund the investigation. Knapp et al. (1972) commented on other investigations about police corruption in other cities stating:

> It seems that the pressure upon policemen, the nature of the job, and the inevitable temptations are similar enough in any large municipal police department at any time to give rise to the kinds of problems found by this commission and its predecessors. (p. 64)

Descriptive titles were provided to police officers dividing them into two corruption categories. Officers who indulged in accepting payments or gratuities were known as the "grass-eaters." Their acts of corruption (receiving free coffee or meals, for instance) were not as serious as the acts of the second group. Grass-eaters might accept payoffs from the public for considerations in return, but they were not known to be aggressive in finding these gratuities or bribes. Sigler and Dees (1988) studied the public perception of corruption similar to that of the grass-eaters during this commission investigation. Their question was whether the public believed that officers were corrupt when receiving small or petty gratuities such as free coffee or discounts on meals.

Their definition of petty corruption was the unsolicited gratuities by a law enforcement officer. They opined that corruption could only be defined by the society in which officers work. For example, what would be corruption in Chicago might not be considered corruption in New York City. They also reported that accepting gratuities might tend to affect the officer's self-esteem or ruin his reputation. Their study occurred in Reno, NV, where randomly chosen citizens (n = 116) were contacted for a seven-question survey. The results of their survey revealed the following: 43.1% (n = 50) agreed that officers should accept petty gratuities, 56% (n = 65) disagreed; 59.5% (n = 69) believed that officers who accepted gratuities provided favorable considerations for those who provide the gratuity, 37.1% (n = 43) disagreed; 14.7% (n = 17) believed that officers should provide special considerations for citizens who gave them gratuities, 81.9% disagreed; 48.3% (n = 56) would provide officers with small gratuities, 47.4% (n = 55) reported they would not; 44.3% (n = 51) reported if they provided gratuities they would expect a special consideration from the officer, 52.2% (n = 60) would not expect a consideration; 50.4% (n = 58) believed that officers should not be permitted to accept small gratuities, 46.1% (n = 53) believed that there should be limits placed upon the acceptance of gratuities; lastly, 18.3% (n = 21) stated that officers should be allowed to accept whereas 39.1% (n = 45) stated that officers should be allowed to accept discounted meals. 42.6% (n = 49) did not respond to these questions (Sigler & Dees, 1988). Sigler and Dees (1988) showed that there were both agreement and disagreement about the acceptance of petty corruption. Conversely, the more aggressive corrupt officers were known as the "meat-eaters." It should be noted that the grass-eaters group was larger than the meat-eaters. However the meat-eaters would aggressively seek out those willing to make higher payoffs for their considerations later on. Loyalty was the motivating factor for the meat-eaters. Once joining the group to collect higher amounts of money, the grass-eaters found it almost impossible to quit. Commitment to this level of corruption required that the group members remain to preclude *snitching* or informing on the other members. Further, refusing to accept payoffs caused the officer to be shunned within the department's camaraderie. Recall that Officer Serpico refused all payments, which ultimately led to his near death experience during a drug transaction and his subsequent expulsion from the department's confidence.

Also considering the pay scale of officers in 1972, a payment of $5000 or more would equal or greatly exceed a year's pay gained in a matter of minutes. This made it difficult for meat-eaters to quit the group. The largest payoff suspected within the department was $250,000; however, it remains unverified (Knapp et al., 1972).

The Sphere of Influence

Besides the possibility of collecting large amounts of money, there must be some type of influence that drives a police officer to enter into acts of corruption. The most basic influence is the character of the police officer. Many police officers do not engage in acts of serious corruption, although they may indulge in lesser receipts of gratuities as an appreciation for their work. It is common to see police officers receiving coffee and small meals from local businesses. Many citizens desire to reward the officers for their work and never mention or expect to receive a consideration in return. These officers may neutralize their actions to themselves, which enables them to continue accepting gratuities. Sykes and Matza developed the theory of neutralization wherein a person could neutralize their actions and lessen their severity. This can also be described as a method of alleviating feelings of guilt or finding excuses for unacceptable behavior. Sykes and Matza formulated five types of neutralization (as cited in Green, 2007):

1. Denial of any injury to others or themselves. If the act did not produce injury then the old adage of "no harm done" may be applicable. Convincing one's self that no harm existed during an act of corruption would remove the feelings of guilt since the provider would receive a service or consideration in return. This could take the form of payoffs or gratuities.
2. Denial of the victim removes harm since the victims actually deserved what occurred. Denying a victim existed during corruptive misconduct might result in the "ripping off" of illicit drug money from dealers. This might also result in acts of vigilantism.
3. Denial of responsibility places the blame elsewhere and upon the person. Blaming the criminals or those who believe paying-off officers switches the blame and responsibility elsewhere and removes guilt from the officer.

4. The condemnation of the condemners identifies the "hypocrites" in the behavior. Those who criticize or penalize those involved are hypocritical since they may be involved as well. Unscrupulous supervisors may collect payments in excess of the patrol officer's. In this regard, the theory of condemning the supervisor who castigates the corrupt officer again validates the officer's actions.
5. Finally, the most important neutralization for this study is the appeal to higher loyalty, or the group. The sense of loyalty to the group prevents officers from quitting their corruptive behaviors due to fear of reprisals.

Another highlighted influence for police corruption is the environment in which the officer works. Sutherland theorized that crime causation was directly linked to criminal behaviors (as cited in Green, 2007). Therefore, environments where certain behaviors are accepted may tend to influence the officer to receive gratuities or commit acts of bribery or extortion. Knapp et al. (1972) documented the life of an officer in Harlem (South Bronx, NYC). In their example, they listed such behaviors as payoffs, numbers rackets, and narcotics. In contrast to this environment there were the possibilities to score major payments from businessmen in Manhattan.

Into the Depths of Corruption

As stated earlier, many police departments experience or condone the acceptance of minor to moderate gratuities. One widely held philosophy about gratuities addresses the manner in which they are offered. If all officers of a department are offered gratuities on an equal basis then the gratuities may be seen as unthreatening to the department as acts of bribery or *being on the take*. When individual officers are targeted for gratuities then a consideration can be expected. This is when a divisible line separates gratuities and the receipt of bribes. Bribes, which may include large amounts of money provided to the officer, also involves considerations regarding unlawful activities. This is the step many officers take when they enter the depths of corruption.

Knapp et al. (1972) found a wide array of activities that resulted in the bribery of officers in return for special treatment. These activities included gambling, narcotics, prostitution, construction, bars,

Sabbath laws, parking and traffic, tow trucks, seized automobiles, and other areas deemed as miscellany by the commission. This discussion will delve deeper into how various crimes were committed by officers of the New York Police Department.

Gambling

Gambling, with the exception of state gambling lotteries or racetracks, was illegal. Like many forms of crime, the offenders opted to bribe police officers into allowing them to continue their activities. Police officers could opt to *shake down* or extort the offenders promising protection from arrest and prosecution. There are various forms of gambling that can be found today as they existed in New York City at the time of the Knapp investigation. These varieties of gambling included *running numbers*, bookmaking, and dice games. These particular types of gambling were quite popular and often included many participants. *Numbers* is a game similar to the state lottery. Citizens could find the local numbers game in local businesses or apartments located on the first floor of apartment buildings. In this fashion, a citizen could make his or her bet on a number quickly to avoid detection of the police. Participants could bet from $0.25, $0.50 to $1.00 on a number from a single digit to three digits. The odds of winning varied (10-1 to 1000-1) depending on how aggressive the participant was, and the payoffs were from 60-1 to 600-1. The person administering the game could realize at least 40% of the winnings (Knapp et al., 1972). The source of the numbers was the result of various racetracks. With the exception of payoffs or bribes to police officers, there were many arrests at local numbers *spots*. Usually, one man was arrested for the numbers operation leaving the boss of the operation to continue the business. Arrests typically did not have an adverse effect upon the numbers game, leading one to believe that the arrests were demonstrations only of police gambling enforcement efforts. The Knapp investigation did discover that officers were being bribed to protect these games. The following table documents how a typical payoff was conducted (Table 2.2).

Another example of demanding payoffs from numbers games was found when the Borough Plainclothes Unit no longer frequented the borough of Queens. In their stead, the Division Plainclothes Unit demanded not only their payoff amount, but the payoff amount of

Table 2.2 Demonstrative Payoff to Police Officers from a Numbers Game

Division Plainclothes Officers	$750
Borough Plainclothes Officers	$300
Detectives	$196
Precinct Sergeants	$180
Precinct Desk Officers	$60
Precinct Gambling Car	$60
Local Patrol Cars	*$120 (weekly)*
Monthly Payoff Total	$2026

Source: Data obtained from Knapp, W. et al., *The Knapp Commission Report on Police Corruption*, Braziller. New York City, NY, 1972, p. 81.

the Borough Plainclothes Unit as well. The benefit received from these payoffs was protection from all police actions regardless of the level from within the department. This, of course, indicates that corruption climbed high within the department. There were two exceptions to this arrangement; token arrests as described previously (also for arrest quotas) and actions by the Public Morals Administrative Division that sought corrupt officers as well as local offenders. If an arrest was needed to demonstrate, enforcement officers would *flake* local offenders by planting fake evidence on them to support their arrest. *Bookmaking* is similar to running numbers in that it is a variant of that type of gambling. Participants in this gambling scheme are referred to as *bookies* since they are receiving betting information from customers rather than the customers coming to them to place their bets. In one instance, the street bookie will make his rounds to various locations in the neighborhood to collect bets and betting choices. These locations can be almost any type, from apartments to businesses. In general, the customers are financially deficient and make small bets. Since his business is static, the police are aware of his contacts and customers. This requires the street bookie to be on the pad so the local officers can be bribed into cooperation and business can continue. Another well-known type of bookmaking is by telephone. In this instance, a telephone bookie conducts business in a local phone booth (which he changes occasionally) to solicit the bets from customers. These bookies will move their phoning operation randomly throughout the city preventing them from being on the pad. However, upon discovery they can be *scored* by police who then receive their payoff against arrest. An example of payoffs from a telephone bookie resulted in his paying $500 to the arresting officer with a demand that he pay an additional $50 a month for 4 months (Knapp et al., 1972). The high-end of being a bookie involved the use of various electronic devices that could not be discovered by the police. Finally there were card and dice games where large amounts of money could be realized by wealthy players. In some instances players could win as much as $15,000 in one game. In one instance $4,000 was demanded as protection from arrest explaining that, "... the two divisions had thirty plainclothesmen each, all of whom were on the pad" (Knapp et al., 1972, p. 88).

Narcotics

Involvement in narcotics was perhaps the darkest hour of the New York Police Department. Vastly different from the other types of corruption found in the city, the narcotics trade involved high-dollar payments and violence. Thus far, police officers were involved in payoffs and bribery. Their payments were slight with few exceptions. The protection rackets in narcotics enabled traffickers to deal in serious volumes of narcotics and protect their investments by paying off police officers who, in turn, were able to realize big payments. Commander Donald Cawley of the Inspections Division testified, "They have entered into personal associations with narcotics criminals and in some cases have used narcotics. They have given false testimony in court in order to obtain dismissal of the charges against a defendant" (as cited in Knapp et al., 1972, p. 91). Most, if not all, of the corruptive acts were predicated upon conspiracies between the local businessmen or organized criminals. Those police officers who indulged in the underworld of narcotics would commit more serious crimes. Like the gambling offenders who were flaked in order to make an arrest for appearances purposes, narcotics offenders were the victims of flaking and padding as well, where police officers would plant narcotics (or increase the quantity already found on the offender through padding) on the person during pretend arrests. In some instances narcotics were provided to informants as rewards for their assistance in drug investigations. The seriousness of this is obvious since police officers had to criminally possess narcotics through stealing or purchases. Of course the cheaper way was to under-report seizures so that their supply of narcotics would remain static for flaking purposes. This is in violation of the narcotics laws placing the police officers in the same category as the offenders. Once obtained, these items, which included the narcotics, needles, and other drug related items were stored in police lockers located in the precincts. In January 1962, the famous "French Connection" case netted 100 lbs of pure heroin, which was smuggled into New York City from France. This case was documented in the film of the same name; however, the film was largely inaccurate. The results of the case were several arrests and the seizure. Shortly following the seizure, the heroin was reported stolen from the evidence locker at the precinct and believed to be returned to the streets either through sale or flaking and padding offenders.

On the more serious side of their involvement, police officers would go to more serious lengths to protect their interests. Reports to the commission included acts such as kidnapping potential witnesses so that they could not testify at trials. Another such report included the police attempts to find *hit men* to murder potential witnesses for the state. There are no records in the commission report of these incidents occurring; therefore, it is possible that these reports are rumors or false testimony. A more believable report was the hiring of police officers to provide protection for narcotics dealers, therefore protecting their interests.

As previously discussed, police officers could receive large payments from narcotics dealers or offenders. It was not uncommon for offenders to offer payoffs to arresting police officers for a redacted arrest report, lowering the quantity seized or altering evidence to increase the likelihood that the case would be dismissed due to the lack of evidence. The ability of police officers to extort large sums of money from dealers was demonstrated through the efforts of a federal undercover agent. In this case, narcotics investigators raided the dealer's hotel room and found $12,000. The investigators demanded that the dealer give them $10,000 to not arrest him. The most interesting part of this case was the narcotics investigator paid a finder's fee of $1000 to another investigator (Knapp et al., 1972). These instances of extortion and bribery continued netting police officers payoffs in excess of $100,000.

Was the New York Police Department ignoring these acts of high-dollar corruption? During the period of investigation, there were 782 police officers assigned to the Narcotics Division (the remainder were assigned to the Detectives Bureau). It is understandable that the most corruption within the narcotics arena was found in the Narcotics Division. In fact, those who were corrupt were known by their superiors who opted to do nothing. A popular belief among police officers, in general, was the money gained from the narcotics was *dirty money* and unacceptable, even to those on the pad from gambling and other activities. The ignorance of narcotics payoffs and related corruption could be partially explained by the social attitude about drugs in general. The younger people of the city were becoming more tolerant about the possession and use of drugs. That, and the possibility of large profits, lured police officers into participating in this type of corruption.

A final interesting note about flushing out offenders who could pay large amounts was the use of wiretapping. Some offenders extorted by police officers were targeted as potential sources of payments by surveillance efforts. Wiretapping is legal only when a search warrant is issued by the appropriate authority. When wiretapping warrants are not available due to insufficient supporting evidence, police officers would then conduct illegal wiretapping for the purposes of collecting intelligence so that extortion could occur. In one case, investigators wiretapped a suspect's phone and collected enough information to extort the offender of $50,000 (Knapp et al., 1972).

Prostitution

The world of prostitution in New York City existed in various forms. *Brothels* or "houses of ill repute" existed in the city wherein prostitutes would engage customers. In these situations, the "manager" would be a "madam" who hired, fired, and collected payments from the women. There were reports indicating that police officers would request payments to prevent arresting the madam. In one particular instance, a madam was approached by a police sergeant who related a lieutenant wanted $1000 not to arrest her, but he would settle for $500 instead. It appeared, based upon the Knapp Commission report, that extortion was relatively rare in regards to brothels. *Prostitute bars* were another style of prostitution. However since bar owners could lose their licenses to operate, no evidence of extortion or payoffs were found. The last category consisted of *call girls* and *streetwalkers*. As with the prostitute bars, payoffs from these women were not lucrative since most of these offenders possessed little to no money. No information was found to indicate that call girls or streetwalkers were making payoffs to police officers. The primary reasons for this was that police officers believed that it was unduly risky to take money from prostitutes since they were dangerous and unreliable (Knapp et al., 1972).

Construction

As early as 1890, the federal government was concerned with inappropriate practices in the construction trade. The government enacted the Sherman Act that was also referred to as anti-trust laws. The essence of these laws was to provide free and open competition for contractors seeking business opportunities. Later, the government enacted the Federal Trade Commission Act of 1914. Even though antitrust laws are available to remedy trade restraints, the restraints need to be unreasonable, like bid rigging among contractors. The Federal Trade Commission's straight forward description of the purpose of the antitrust laws is, "to protect the process of competition for the benefit of consumers, making sure there are strong incentives for businesses to operate efficiently, keep prices down, and keep quality up" (Federal Trade Commission, 2014, para. 2). Obviously, the antitrust laws come into play before the construction projects begin and do not involve law enforcement. However, to make the connection to the New York Police Department, it is important to understand why construction contractors and police officers became involved in corruption together. One has only to look at the New York City codes for construction to understand the extent to which contractors have to adhere to codes that are applicable to their profession. Presently, the 2015 construction codes for New York City consist of five parts: general provisions, plumbing, mechanical, fuel, and building. Each of these codes provides detailed information about construction requirements. The plumbing code consists of 13 chapters and seven appendices; the mechanical code consists of 15 chapters plus 1 appendix; the fuel code consists of eight chapters plus two appendices; and the building code consists of thirty-three chapters plus eleven appendices (NYC.gov, 2014a). Many construction projects require a permit from the city's building department. Looking at the construction during Knapp era, it would be common for a general contractor to seek as many as 130 permits to complete their project. The number of permits could become prohibitive to timely work. The financial burden of obtaining this number of permits was also challenging and prompted many contractors to disregard various permits and just concentrate upon the more important projects. Aside from the number of permits needed and the cost, some permits seemed odd. In one example provided by the commission, a permit was required from the city to move heavy equipment over a sidewalk. In some cases this was a waste of time since it was a single instance. In the end, the commission described the permit situation as "… the dizzying array of laws, ordinances, and regulations governing construction in the City" (Knapp et al., 1972, p. 125).

The connection between construction and law enforcement became clear; police officers had the responsibility to enforce permits at construction sites. This practice of enforcing permits did not seem to be a law enforcement function since building inspectors held the same responsibility. This double inspection situation also prompted contractors to bribe inspectors as well as police officers thereby doubling the cost of their operations. Contractors believed that it was in their best financial interest to provide payoffs to police officers.

The enforcement scheme used by the New York Police Department included a *conditions man*, or a foot police officer who visited the construction sites to enforce permits and other conditions at the site. This function was then changed to a *summons man* who had a wider variety of responsibilities including inspecting construction sites and issuing summonses for violations. These summonses were issued for improper or missing permits, nonconformity to the permits, and the lack of adherence of other various city ordinances aside from the permits in question. The amount of construction and all of the permits required by the contractors in New York City could be daunting for foot police officers to review and enforce. Commission investigators learned that most police officers assigned to this duty merely recorded permit numbers and let it go at that. Basically, the police officers were not doing their jobs. Once again, believing that corruption trickled down from leadership to worker, ignoring enforcement responsibilities made corruption more prevalent. The mode of corruption was payoffs to police officers in patrol cars, and the amount of the payoff was commensurate with the size and price of the construction project. The average amount paid to patrol officers was $166.00 (Knapp et al., 1972) depending upon individual circumstances of the project. The New York Police Department halted the use of police officers to enforce both permits and ordinances and returned them to more law enforcement related activities. The city attempted to concentrate upon contractors who were offering these bribes. However, at the time of the commission investigation the city had yet to place this enforcement plan in place.

At this time, an interesting comment needs to be made about the value of the U.S. dollar in 1972 as compared to the 2013 U.S. dollar. Many payoffs to police officers were in the $50–$100 range, with some payoffs being much larger. Recall that some payments in the gambling corruption schemes could net a police officer as much as $50,000. Based upon the Consumer Price Index, the value of the 1972 U.S. dollar was $5.57 as compared to the dollar in 2013 (MeasuringWorth.com, 2014). The following table demonstrates other relative values germane to 1972 corruption placing those values into perspective in 2013 (Table 2.3).

Bars

Alcohol remains a very sought after commodity. Because of this bars, lounges, and other establishments have been targets for graft or bribery and many proprietors have paid so that they could retain their licenses. Along with construction, businesses that provided alcoholic beverages were one of the top areas where corruption was found.

Table 2.3 Relative Value of 1972 U.S. Dollar to the Year 2013

EXAMPLE OF REPORTED PAYOFF TO OFFICERS ($)	RELATIVE VALUE IN 2013 ($)
50	278
100	557
500	2,780
1000	5,570
10,000	55,700
50,000	278,000
100,000	557,000

Source: MeasuringWorth.com, Seven ways to compute the relative value of a U.S. dollar amount—1774 to present, 2014, Retrieved from http://www.measuringworth.com/uscompare/

Drinking establishments were also under strict guidelines by law, and infractions could result in the loss of their licenses or criminal charges and penalties. In addition to drinking establishments, restaurants served alcohol as well. However the investigation did not develop evidence that restaurants were soliciting or receiving bribes from police officers. The commission did note, however, that restaurants were providing police officers with other gratuities such as meals, drinks, and gifts during holidays. In addition to legal lounges, bars, and other venues, there were also *juice bars* that sold alcohol during the times the legal venues were closed. Similar to construction enforcement, bars and other establishments were placed under the control of police officers. In this case, the licenses were open to inspection and supervision of the patrol sergeants; however, this was eventually transferred to the responsibility of plainclothes officers or detectives. As with other areas of corruption, bar owners made weekly or biweekly payments to police officers who in turn protected them from license revocation. Part of this was the result of extortion where police officers, namely sergeants, would threaten to make false allegations of health violations against the bar with the possibility of revocation of the license. There were also instances of outright extortion where sergeants or detectives would plant purported drug evidence in the bar or threaten the owner with false allegations of various violations, which could lead to the revocation of licenses. In one instance, commission investigators were mistaken as police officers and were offered the usual pad money. It was not uncommon for police officers to receive up to $500 for their protection. Many unsavory occurrences, such as brawls among customers, drew the attention of the licensing authorities. Police officers took advantage of these incidents by taking payments from bar owners so that arrest reports would not reach the State Liquor Authority.

Unlicensed venues, such as after-hours clubs, catered to the homosexual population in the East Village area. These clubs, which served alcohol, provided sex locations for almost 700 men in one evening (Knapp et al., 1972). Police officers who were bribed could receive $2,000 a month from the more popular clubs. On various occasions, patrols would drive past these clubs where obvious crimes or violations were occurring without taking any preventive or enforcement actions.

Parking and Traffic

To provide some perspective of traffic in New York City, there are currently approximately 10,000 taxi cabs that service the city. Many of these taxis are located in Manhattan where people prefer not to drive due to the concentrated traffic conditions. It is unknown how many cars, trucks, or buses travel the roads of the city during a single day. Many businesses rely upon available parking spots so they can deliver or pickup their merchandise or other types of property. In some areas of the city it is common to see *double parking*. Mostly found in the boroughs' residential areas, residents seek parking spots near their homes, and it is not uncommon to fail in this search. Therefore, they may elect to park next to a parked car extending their car further into the street; this practice is illegal. To further aggravate this situation, there is also *alternate side of the street parking*. In order to clean the streets, the city requires all cars on one side of the street to move to the opposite side of the street or elsewhere. Parking can be a premium in the city on most days of the week. Is it practical for citizens and businessmen to voluntarily pay parking tickets for their convenience? In 1972 a parking violation would cost a person $25 for the violation and $50 for the towing charge. Using today's data, parking violations can be quite costly. The former $25 parking fee in 2013 is $139 and the former $50 towing fee is now $278. Today, parking violations are an average of $115 for parking in various restricted zones (NYC.gov, 2014c). Corruption for parking violations may seem trivial in nature, but the need for parking trucks or cars for business purposes can be an expensive proposition.

One restriction that businesses faced was the hours in which parking was disallowed. In Manhattan, parking was prohibited between 8:00 a.m. and 6:00 p.m. A violation would immediately result in towing. Since parking was such a commodity, business owners were happy to pay pad money to police officers rather than having their businesses suffer from delinquent deliveries. The commission found one instance where a bar owner paid police officers so that his customers could double and *triple* park their cars to frequent his establishment (Knapp et al., 1972). Oddly, it was found that some unscrupulous business owners actually maintained books where they recorded the expenses for the illegal parking arrangements they had with the local patrols. If a business opted not to pay pad money to the police and paid their violations, fines could amount to in excess of $50,000 a year. In contrast to the citizen parking issues, police officers blatantly parked illegally in tow-away zones and other restricted areas. Their rationale was that the city was to afford them parking and, since parking was scarce by the precinct, they were within their authority to park elsewhere regardless of prohibitions.

Moving violations are also very common. For those who do not rely upon their cars for their livelihood, a moving violation would be nothing more than a fine, and in some cases, towing the car as a seizure. This is not the case for those who do rely upon their vehicles for their livelihood. For example, many drivers are required to possess a commercial driver's license to transport property or passengers. Taxi, truck, limousine, and other types of professional drivers cannot afford to have their vehicles towed, and paying fines for moving violations could result in their licenses being suspended or revoked. This can now breed corruption since police officers are in control of who gets fined. New York City, the largest city in the United States, which currently has over 8,000,000 citizens (not counting those who are just visiting or driving through) is a prime hunting ground for any unscrupulous police officers who may want to make extra income from pad money through extortion or bribery. This is exactly what was happening in the city in the late 1960s and into the 1970s. Police officers were known to offer non-law enforcement services for nominal payments such as assisting drivers with their cars or offering to ignore moving violations. Aside from ticketing drivers for moving violations, police officers were involved in a rather unique corruption scheme. Police department personnel were found to enter into a conspiracy with car rental companies to sell stolen car data. The rental companies in turn would attempt to gain business from these car owners.

To sum up this discussion of parking and traffic, towing was also part of the corruption scheme for many police officers. Towing rates themselves would not net officers any money since the rates were controlled by law and were not expensive. However, this did not prevent officers from recognizing that many disabled cars needed repairs or tows. Tow truck drivers, aside from being called for assistance, would patrol the streets looking for business and then offer their services. In their haste they would commit moving violations, which would be ignored by police officers for a price. In many instances tow truck drivers would be called by police officers who found a traffic accident or disabled car and pay the officers about $25 for their tip. The following finding from the commission leaves an interesting view about tow truck corruption:

> When police payoffs are made by towing companies, those companies are left free to harass and browbeat motorists who have been involved in accidents, after signing them up at the scene for repair work which will be billed at rates inflated at least enough to cover the payoffs. (Knapp et al., 1972, p. 162)

When tow trucker drivers experienced reluctance from drivers, responding police officers would assist in either convincing the driver to use this "great company" or threaten the driver with traffic violations. In the end, the police received money.

Miscellaneous Areas of Corruption Not Fully Developed

Is that all there was to the corruption? Based upon what was found by the commission, it is apparent that police officers were willing to bribe almost anyone. The commission did not have time or the resources to continue their investigation of every complaint of corruption. There were additional areas where information was obtained wherein it was indicated that police officers bribed or extorted those involved in what was termed "Miscellany." One of the most shocking instances of corruption was the theft of property from the dead. A DOA (dead on arrival) was a decedent found at a crime scene or other location. Claims were made that the police officers would rummage through the victim's pockets for valuables, such as money or jewelry. The dead also provided police officers with the opportunity to burglarize their homes by searching the scene or using the victim's keys to steal property. It was expected that many people, rather than trust banks, would keep their money in their homes instead.

Aside from DOA corruption, there are various other areas where corruption was found, although the list is not exclusive. *Loan sharks*, those who make loans at exaggerated and illegal rates of interest (sometimes followed up with violence), were reportedly part of the corruption scheme. Here, police officers could make money through payments from the loan sharks by agreeing not to arrest them for their crimes. Reported amounts paid to police officers ranged between $10 and $100 either on a weekly basis or one time basis. Since loan sharks are not licensed to provide loans at interest rates for recovery of the funds, those who receive these loans are not legally bound to make payments. It is for this reason that violence or threats may be used to force recipients to make their payments, oftentimes within unreasonable time frames. An example of the violent end of a loan shark loan can be found in the *New York Post* where a reputed slum lord was murdered for defaulting on a massive loan of more than $1,000,000. The victim was murdered through asphyxiation and his body was burned (Celona, Schram, & Golding, 2014). This type of example was common in 1972 as it is today. *Hijacking*, or the illegal seizure of another's property, was another area of interest by the commission, although the only information received was too vague for further investigation. Again, as in other types of corruption, police officers were either reportedly involved in a hijacking conspiracy or approached and paid upon their appearance at the scene.

Whenever the Bronx district attorney announced arrests or indictments, the alleged payoffs of police officers were more believable than unsubstantiated reports. In the next category of corruption, police officers were indicted for their involvement in an *auto theft ring*. The allegations were that police officers participated directly with the offenders by acting as guards against discovery (their status as police officers would provide a believable cover story) or participated in dismantling cars for resale purposes. Police officers and detectives were offered approximately $2,000 for their assistance. This investigation resulted in the guilty pleas of the detectives (Knapp et al., 1972).

In connection with DOA thefts, informant police officers provided information to the commission about *theft from burglary scenes*. To provide first-hand information, the following statement was provided to the Knapp Commission investigators:

> Me and my partner went in the back of the building [where] the door was open. We went in. There was about six or seven radio cars out front. A lot of cops was (sic) inside. Everybody was stuffing clothing down their pants, in their shirt, up their sleeves. (p. 186)

This type of information from trustworthy sources prompted surveillances where further acts of thefts were observed. Interestingly, police officers would steal property from private residences as well from businesses while loading the stolen goods into patrol cars. Later, the stolen property would be transferred into the police officer's privately owned cars, usually parked adjacent or near the precinct.

Pistol permits can be purchased in New York City, but not as easily as in 1972. Currently, aside from the standard application of identification and fees (a total of $431.50), the applicant needs to provide the New York Police Department with a letter of necessity. This letter covers both carrying a weapon as well as a premises permit (NYC.gov, 2014b). In 1972 the application fee was $20. However, it was found that applicants would be informed that upon paying their $20 fee they were to also provide an additional fee of $100. It was understood that this additional fee was to be provided to the precinct commander who made the decision about approving the application. Gun dealers were not exempt from this practice either. Dealers were required to provide pad money to either police officer bagmen or to a representative of the pistol bureau. In regards to the precinct commander's decision to approve an application, they were required to personally interview each applicant. Knowing this, applicants who desired a permit could be influenced to pay the commander $100 for the approval.

There are many people who opt to believe in the predictions or advice of *fortune tellers*. These people could come from religious homes, the elderly, and other suggestible backgrounds. Like other acts of corruption, police officers participate in payoffs and bribery therefore preventing the fortune tellers from being arrested for theft. In this area, the primary police officers involved in bribery were detectives assigned to the Pickpocket and Confidence squad. The offenders providing fortune telling were involved in the *Gypsy* confidence games where the confidence of victims was obtained through promises of future information for various sums of money. Obviously, many of the "fortunes" did not come true and victims were apt to report the theft of their money to the police. It is for these reasons the offenders bribe detectives. The primary victims in these schemes were the elderly. One very common scheme was to offer a victim the *Gypsy blessing* where *curses* are fended off by the *spiritual advisor.* Victims provided their advisors with money, which was then placed into a bag and returned to the victim as a blessing who later learned that the bag had been switched for one with paper inside. The theft from victims would vary to as much as $40,000 (Knapp et al., 1972). The unscrupulous detectives would receive 15% of the thefts. Finally, perhaps the most serious acts of bribery occurred in court. Police officers were paid to alter their testimonies so that defendants could benefit from lesser sentences or dismissed charges. In one case, with the assistance of police officer, a lawyer negotiated bribery to judges for $10,000 for a defendant who had stolen a $250,000 check.

A Broad Look at the Knapp Report

The information that is contained in the Knapp Commission report is quite extensive. Clearly, the degree to which corruption and misconduct occurred throughout the department spanned from individual officers to the groups of officers and to the administration. No information was available to indicate how many officers were corrupt. From reading the report, the wide array of corruption was not correlated to officers by name. It appeared that many officers who decided to engage in corrupt behaviors could do so entirely on their own. However it was seen that refusing membership into organized groups of officers could lead to the end of one's career or death. Officer Frank Serpico (n.d.) was able to sum up the existence of police officers in the New York Police Department during the Knapp Commission era by stating, "An honest cop still can't find a place to go and complain without fear of recrimination. The blue wall will always be there because the system supports it" (n.p.). The report also provides a view of how the city reacted to law enforcement. Typically, most citizens had no involvement with the department other than for being involved in various crimes as suspects, witnesses, or victims. By and large, the citizen did not possess sufficient finances to payoff officers, therefore most corruption was targeted against businesses or the more lucrative crime ventures such as narcotics. Without the proper leadership from the department administration, corruption was found in almost every aspect of the officer's professional life. As the Knapp Commission reported, corruption was wide spread throughout the city.

References

Celona, L., Shram, J., & Golding, B. (2014, January 7). Slain slum lord owned more than $1M to loan sharks. *New York Post*. Retrieved from: http://nypost.com/2014/01/07/slain-slumlord-fought-to-the-end-was-asphyxiated-in-kidnap-van/

Federal Trade Commission. (2014). The anti-trust laws. Retrieved from: http://www.ftc.gov/tips-advice/competition-guidance/guide-antitrust-laws/antitrust-laws.

Garner, B. (2014). *Black's Law Dictionary* (10th ed.). Boston, MA: Thomson. Retrieved from: http://thelawdictionary.org/hearsay-evidence/

Green, G. (2007). *Techniques of neutralization*. In L. Salinger (Ed.), *Encyclopedia of white collar & corporate crime* (pp. 798–799). Thousand Oaks, CA: SAGE Publications. doi: 10.4135/9781412914260.n423

Knapp, W., Monserrat, J., Sprizzo, J., Thomas, F., & Vance, C. (1972). *The Knapp Commission report on police corruption*. New York, NY: Braziller.

MeasuringWorth.com. (2014). Seven ways to compute the relative value of a U.S. dollar amount—1774 to present. Retrieved from: http://www.measuringworth.com/uscompare/

NYC.gov. (2014a). 2014 Construction codes. Retrieved from: http://www.nyc.gov/html/dob/html/codes_and_reference_materials/2014_construction_code.shtml

NYC.gov. (2014b). Instructions to handgun license applicants. Retrieved from: http://www.nyc.gov/html/nypd/downloads/pdf/permits/HandGunLicenseApplicationFor msComplete.pdf

NYC.gov. (2014c). Violation codes, fines, rules, & regulations. Retrieved from: http://www.nyc.gov/html/dof/html/parking/violation_codes.shtml

NYPD. New York's Finest. (2015). Retrieved from: http://www.nyc.gov/html/nypd/html/faq/faq_police.shtml#1

Police Athletic League. (2014). Retrieved from: http://www.palnyc.org/800-PAL-4KIDS/History.aspx

Serpico, F. (n.d.). BrainyQuote.com. Retrieved from: http://www.brainyquote.com/ quotes/authors/f/frank_serpico.html

Sigler, R. T., & Dees, T. M. (1988). Public perception of petty corruption in law enforcement. *Journal of Police Science and Administration, 16*(1), 14–19.

3
The Mollen Commission Investigation

> Its most prevalent form is not police taking money to accommodate criminals by closing their eyes to illegal activities such as bookmaking, as was the case twenty years ago, but police acting as criminals, especially in connection with the drug trade.
>
> **Mollen Commission**

This opening statement by the Mollen Commission set the stage for the depth of corruption that existed 20 years later. Inasmuch as the Knapp Commission found "… corruption to be widespread" it did not discover that many police officers of the New York Police Department were criminals since most acts of corruption were based upon greed and conspiracy. Now the police officers were more-hardened criminals, from burglars and thieves to murderers. As was seen at the end of the Knapp Commission investigation, many efforts and policies were put in place to combat and prevent corruption. At the beginning of the investigation, the New York Police Department was reactive to corruption and later turned proactive. Did it really become sufficiently proactive and turn the tide of corruption? How could the department explain the new approach to corruption when its officers were now the criminals? Responsibility, accountability, and training were the new efforts to prevent corruption; however, it is apparent that these new efforts failed somewhere between 1972 and 1994.

The department administration placed the blame for corruption squarely upon the rogue officer who acted independently. These were considered to be isolated incidents of corruption and no organized groups of officers existed to benefit from their greed. This was considered to be the main motivation. The new commission rebuked these claims finding that they were not only wrong, but sadly misunderstood as to their complicity in criminal enterprise (Mollen, Baer, Evans, Lankler, & Tyler, 1994).

As of July 24, 1992, the newly formed Mollen Commission began its 22-month investigation into systemic corruption. An immediate conclusion by the commission concerned the resistance by police officers to divulge information about corruption. It is general knowledge that there is a code of silence that prohibits honest officers from reporting the misdeeds of others. Once broken, the officer would be subject to castigation with the loss of trust by others. Recalling Officer Serpico's experience, it was suspected that he almost lost his life for revealing the corruption of others. Remember that the New York Police Department attempted democratic reform. This proactive reform was hopefully going to reduce the incidents of misbehavior in the department. Ivković and Shelley (2010) found that the stronger the silence the weaker the culture of integrity would be. Further, the implementation of policy changes would be hindered as well. Therefore, it is not surprising that officers chose not to report to their superiors. There were other reasons discovered by the commission that explained the lack of reporting, such as disinterested supervisors, lax accountability, and the abandonment of responsibility and accountability. Further, as reflected in the opening quote, police officers were now becoming the criminals, and not alone; there were now organized groups of officers engaging in criminal activities. Because of the loosening of proactive efforts from 1972, the department permitted the proactive systems to fail, or as described by Mollen, "virtually collapse." The seemingly cooperative nature of the department in 1972 apparently shied away from bad publicity. The more corruption that is found, the worse the organization is perceived. So in order to prevent this from happening, the department became defensive and began hiding the new form of corruption, that of criminality. Mollen et al. (1994) summed up this new situation by stating, "This abandonment of effective anticorruption efforts did more than avoid public exposure of corruption, it fueled it" (p. 3).

How Police Corruption Has Changed

Changes occurred in how corruption was perceived in New York City. Perhaps the major area where corruption now resided was the narcotics trade. Formerly, many police officers considered narcotics payoffs as dirty money, something to stay away from. It was in a different realm than accepting payoffs for parking or other considerations for citizens. Now, between 1992 and 1994, the narcotics trade was the staple of the corrupt police officer. In fact, the money gained from this type of corruption was no longer considered to be "dirty." The manner in which payments and drugs were received also changed. Rather than being paid to ignore aspects of narcotic transactions, the police officers involved opted to steal from dealers, form organized groups for gain, or develop long-term relationships with drug traffickers (Mollen et al., 1994). In short, the new drug dealers in New York City wore uniforms with badges. This new schematic of the narcotics trade also changed the face of the victims. Once the police officers switched sides, the victims, formerly the drug dealers and users, were now the citizens who were not involved in many crimes. Once the drug dealers victimized their neighborhoods with tentative cooperation of the police; now the police were enabling this victimization with some degree of impunity. This new wave of corruption was in the public eye, which then resulted in resentment and cynicism in the community. This type of attitude toward the police is nothing new given the history of law enforcement in the United States. Carr, Napolitano, and Keating (2007) studied the citizens' reaction to policing, namely youths. Due to the environment and experiences with the police, youths possessed negative attitudes and opinions of the police. They also learned that since the 1970s, African American citizens fostered distrust of the police more so than the white communities. In their collation of attitudes toward the police, 223 respondents were surveyed of which 61.8% of the population reported negative opinions of the police. Of these opinions the highest percentages were in the "police as ineffective" (15.2%) and "negative interaction described" (18.4%) categories. The Mollen Commission did not conduct surveys but rather collected information from their investigative efforts. To mirror the data collected from Carr et al. (2007), the commission reported, "It breeds a sense of abandonment and hostility that poisons relations between the community and corrupt and honest cops alike" (Mollen et al., 1994, p. 15).

Police officers maintain a status of power and authority. Recall that authority is the unqualified entitlement to be obeyed due to the position held. Power is the ability to overcome resistance. In the world of policing, the laws provide police officers with the authority of enforcement with the power to, in some cases, physically ensure compliance. During the Mollen Commission investigation, corrupt police offers used their given powers to promote and protect drug dealers from prosecution. This protection came at a price. Along with these newly held powers, the characteristics of corruption changed as well. Formerly, "the grass eaters," or the officers who opted for bribes and other pay-offs, were the majority of the corrupt. Now, 20 years later, the meat eaters now ruled as the majority of the corrupt segment of the department (Mollen et al., 1994).

One point of good news did exist in the post-Knapp era. Unlike the police department administration in the 1960s and 1970s, which made efforts to hide corruption, the Mollen Commission found that this trend had reversed. With the exception of some command personnel, the administration was found to be free of corruption at the higher ranks.

Organized Corruption

Among the new types of corruption that existed for the Mollen Commission, there was one aspect that had changed for the better since the Knapp investigation. Previously, payments, known as pads, were found to be part of organized efforts. Recall that patrol officers, sergeants, and higher ranking supervisors would all partake of the pad money in consideration of the citizen's desires. However, the Mollen Commission found that this type of organized corruption did not exist to its previous extent. In fact, the police officers involved in the theft of money from drug dealers were the minority; police officers who acted alone. As good as this appeared to be, the good news ended here. Other acts of corruption involved organized groups of police officers. These groups were known as the *crews*. Aside from benefiting from their corruptive actions, the members of the crews would work in concert to not only receive their rewards, but also to protect other crew members and to assist them in their efforts as well. The number of crew members varied. Their actions were very aggressive in that they planned unlawful raids, forcibly entered and looted narcotics sites, and split their proceeds according to their agreed upon principles. For example, a crew of 8–10 police officers from the 73rd precinct worked together to unlawfully raid various known narcotics locations during the years of 1988–1992. There were times when the majority of police officers in this crew would hold surreptitious meetings at an abandoned coffin factory, where they would plan their future unlawful activities. Other crews, such as one from the Bronx, would frequently burglarize known narcotics locations and brutally beat local residents along with suspects. Later part of this discussion will address acts of police brutality. To accomplish their unlawful ventures, the crew members would misuse their positions as police officers by using coded communications, using department resources (such as cars and radios), and generating leads to identify new targets. Not only did these new crews heighten the amount of corruption, they also directly involved the department as a resource. It was important that all crew members or partners agreed to this type of behavior. New partners or police officers could be tested for their reliability and trustworthiness. Agreements to share the *take* were either by direct agreement or by the mere understanding that the proceeds would be divided amongst the participants.

The Gold Mines

The manner in which these police officers would identify potential targets was to obtain information from dealers or other suspects. Once obtained, the police officers would commit burglaries, thefts, or robberies. Eventually, the police officers learned the trade of a narcotics dealer and how to hide their expensive stashes of drugs. Since most of the narcotics locations were in the lower-economic areas, police officers learned that better security meant hidden drugs. Apartments in these buildings would be secured by high-grade locks whereas the law abiding building tenants would have the standard lock on their homes. These high-grade locks could be opened by using a *felony key*, or the key to an apartment which was seized during an unlawful search and seizure. The ultimate search inside of these apartments would cause great damage as the police officers would damage or destroy personal property or the structure of the apartment. If the narcotics were found, what were the dealers to do? Call the police and complain about their drugs being stolen?

The Code

Police officers who were receiving regular payments from suspects had to devise a way to prevent their exposure to the department, namely, the Internal Affairs Division (IAD). To accomplish this, police officers used codes to announce the presence of IAD investigators. One example of this code was "W0-10," which translated to "Watch out 7 + 3," or be aware that investigators were present in the 73rd precinct areas (Mollen et al., 1994). Other tactics used to prevent detection were the manners of getting paid. First, police officers could not afford to be paid directly from dealers in a public area. This would enable the IAD investigators to observe the transaction and arrest the officers. Rather, dealers would drop payments in various locations in their precincts for the police officers to retrieve. In this way, if the drop was in a local store, a police officer would only be seen departing with a paper bag. In some instances, the police officers would share responsibilities for their corruptive actions while leaving the suspects with some drugs or money to buy their silence. Silence has always been an ally for the corrupt police officer. Cops would not rat on cops. Rothwell and Baldwin (2007) found that organized groups, or work groups of uniformed officers or investigators, were more prone to experience unexpected circumstances with the community or suspects. In some of these encounters, various actions may be taken that are inappropriate or unlawful, which require codes of silence among the officers. Reciprocal silence is important for the cohesion of police officers who find themselves involved in questionable actions that may bring discredit or prosecution upon themselves.

Categories of Corruption

Like the Knapp Commission, the Mollen Commission noted various categories of corruption. However, now the categories included more heinous crimes such as armed robberies and murder. It appeared that there was no limit to which the police officers would go to gain financial benefit from their actions. Aside from the desire for money, property, or drugs, some of the police officers engaged in acts of corruption for the sheer enjoyment and excitement of it. This excitement came from conducting raids (legal or illegal) and *booming doors* as was described by police officers interviewed by the commission. Booming doors was the term used to describe illegal entries into suspected drug locations. These raids were conducted without probable cause or search warrants. Depending upon the precinct, the term may change to *doing doors* which had the same meaning. The commission found five distinct categories of patterns of corruption. These categories included theft, protecting drug dealers, police officers as drug dealers, perjury and false reporting, and police brutality (or acts of random violence) (Mollen et al., 1994, p. 22).

Brutality and Violence

The most severe pattern of corruption in this category list is police brutality or acts of violence. The question here is why did police officers engage in these acts of violence when they were able to benefit from bribery, extortion, or theft? Mollen et al. (1994) found that the Knapp Commission did not address brutality or violence at all. The Knapp Commission report centered upon corruptive acts that garnered the police officers money, and in some cases, property or drugs. Here, the Mollen Commission faces the issue of brutality. The Mollen Commission also opined that any investigating body would be remiss in their responsibilities if they did not suspect or collect claims of violence and brutality. The following observation was made by the commission, "We found that corruption and brutality are often linked in a variety of ways – and should no longer be artificially separated by police managers, corruption fighters, and policy-makers" (p. 44). Did the Knapp Commission treat brutality and violence as minor parts of the identified types of corruption? Considering the absence of brutality in the Knapp report it will remain unknown as to what extent it was involved in corruption. It can be conceded that violence is part of police strategies when protecting themselves and the public. Police officers are confronted with a tremendous variety of crimes, many of which are inherently dangerous. At some point there must be a distinct line between justified police force and acts of brutality. To provide a picture of police misconduct due to violence, Packman (2010) compiled statistics from the second quarter of 2010 addressing misconduct in the United States. In this study, 23.3% of police officers were involved in acts of excessive force and 4.8% were involved in acts of assault. Of the excessive force cases, physical assault occurred in 62% of the cases and firearms were used in 13%. Thirteen percent of the excessive force incidents involved fatalities, and of these, 60% were due to firearms. Although not specifically identifying acts of brutality, this study supports the Mollen Commission's belief that brutality and acts of violence needed to be investigated in all corruption investigations.

Acts of brutality and violence occurred mostly in the crime ridden sections of the city. Further, there were inadequate records reflecting the frequency in which it occurred due to the reluctance of police officers to discuss or report it. Specific acts of brutality, which included murder, also involved threats of death. Three instances of brutality were documented by the commission. In one case, a drug dealer was shot in the stomach by a police officer and robbed of his drugs; another police officer shoved his gun in a dealer's mouth threatening to "blow his brains out," and a third police officer threatened to have dogs attack a dealer in order to get his cooperation. The commission then conducted a study of 234 police officers who were identified as most likely to become corrupt based upon allegations of force against them. The conclusion was that these officers were five times more likely to have at least five or more allegations of unnecessary force against them (Mollen et al., 1994, p. 46).

Aside from the police officers, supervisors were also found to tolerate brutality or excessive force by turning a blind eye. This was based upon the type of attitudes the supervisors possessed. For example, there were such attitudes as the force was deserved or there was nothing wrong with a bit of force in order to enforce laws. In the end, the department paid the literal price for brutality and excessive force. According to the commission, the city paid millions of dollars to litigants as a result of law suits. Not only did this affect the city financially, it also resulted in further distrust by the community when criminal charges of assault or murder were brought against officers.

Perjury and Falsification

Another category of corruption was the *perjury* and *falsification* of records and reports by police officers to cover or rationalize their actions. Police officers possess the appearance of honesty when they report details of crimes or crime scenes. They produce a variety of documents that are based upon their veracity. For example, searches and seizures are predicated upon the application of an affidavit containing detailed and accurate information based upon the officer's observations and evidence. Other forms of falsification can be reports, records, and verbal testimony. Both the Knapp and Mollen Commission investigations found that committing perjury in court was also known as *testilying*.

The significance of committing perjury at trial is oftentimes the word of a police officer who may sway the conclusions of the grand jury, trial jury, or even the conclusion by judges during bench trials (judge alone). Mollen et al. (1994) interviewed large numbers of potential witnesses regarding this issue. It was their conclusion that perjury and falsification was probably the most commonly found form of corruption in the police department. One interesting occurrence that can protect police officers from committing perjury is the plea deal. Partially supported by false documents, defendants had the option to plea to lesser charges so as not to face a criminal trial and a potentially stiff sentence. To view a larger picture of the plea deal (or plea bargain) the Bureau of Justice Assistance (BJA) (2011) reported that in 2003 federal prosecutions were settled in 75,573 trials or by the acceptance of a plea bargain. Ninety-five percent, or 71,794 cases were disposed by accepting a plea of guilty thereby preventing the need for a trial. It was also estimated that 90%–95% of both state and federal trials are disposed of through the use of the plea deal. Those who opt for trial will usually face harsher sentences than those who plead guilty.

There are ways that police officers could falsely support their actions as legal. One example was police officers would provide false probable cause or suspicion to conduct raids of suspected drug locations. The *hot pursuit* doctrine permits police officers to forcibly enter to apprehend offenders and seize evidence. Once inside the premises, the officer could claim the *plain view* doctrine to seize evidence. Therefore, once inside of a suspected drug location using false hot pursuit, the officer could claim that evidence was in plain view that permits its seizure as long as the police officer is present legally. Other tactics were the consent of the suspect for a search or the suspect dropped or threw away evidence during a chase. In the end, the suspect's version of what occurred was against the word of the "honest cop." Aside from seizing evidence or conducting illegal searches, police officers would also falsely report their excessive force by adding the phrase "resisting arrest" to their arrest report. This would permit police officers to commit acts of brutality or violence upon suspects, informants, or witnesses. Acts of *vigilantism* were committed through the use of falsification. Some police officers did not agree with the department rules, policies, or procedures and opted to change the law to suit their personal beliefs on how the law should be carried out. Mollen et al. (1994) saw these tactics as shortcuts that "… not only violate basic constitutional rights – they allow police officers, rather than the legislature, to make the law and enforce their own brand of street justice" (p. 39). There were other reasons for falsifications of arrests or searches. These reasons were known as *collars for dollars* or *trading collars*. It was known that arrests and evidence seizures oftentimes resulted in extra income for the police officers through overtime pay or some more lucrative assignments or promotions, like patrolman to detective. The trading collars scheme was a way to help other officers who needed or desired overtime pay or "points" toward promotions.

Attitudes were also considered concerning the use of perjury or falsification. Supervisors were found to believe that there was nothing wrong with committing perjury or falsifying information when trying superseding the civil rights of known criminals. Some police officers called these practices "doing God's work" and "What's wrong with that? They're guilty!" (Mollen et al., 1994, p. 41). Supervisors were rarely held accountable for these behaviors committed by their officers. Furthermore, the commission failed to find any instance where supervisors were sanctioned for this type of corruption. In fact, the commission failed to find any instances of IAD-initiated investigations concerning perjury or falsification of information.

Theft

As found during the Knapp Commission investigation, theft was a common type of corruption. Most of the corruption in 1972 was based upon greed. This greed motivated the police officers to take bribes from suspects or extort both suspects and law abiding citizens as well as stealing what was available to them. In line with other patterns of corruption in 1994, theft was also predicated upon threats or violence. The most common method was the *shakedowns* where officers would demand money from suspects. Tantamount to robbery, police officers would threaten suspects with arrest and prosecution to force the suspect to give them money. One police officer, who was cooperating with the commission, reported that his weekly goal was between $300 and $500. However, during holidays it was common for him to collect between $1,500 and $2,500 a week (Mollen et al., 1994, p. 22). In order to prevent complaints and department investigations, police officers would do their best to leave their targets happy after the theft. The following philosophy supported this tactic, "… if you left a drug dealer happy after stealing from him, he would not only be unlikely to complain, but would come to accept police shakedowns as a routine 'tax' or cost of doing business" (Mollen et al., 1994, p. 23).

Theft from patrol assignments, or *radio runs* also occurred quite frequently. Patrols were sent to a wide variety of crimes throughout the city. The investigations would require police officers to enter apartments and houses to complete their work. This provided them with the opportunity to search the premises and steal what was available to them. Not only did they steal from a crime scene, but drugs were stolen from the bodies of deceased suspects. Other police officers and supervisors who apparently observed this behavior failed to take any actions or make reports to the department. In the absence to radio runs, some officers fabricated their own runs to the most likely locations where money, property, or drugs could be stolen.

It is interesting to note the benefits from stealing from crime scenes, radio run assignments, and raids. Mollen et al. (1994) was able to determine that the largest score realized during a raid was $100,000. It was not uncommon for police officers to steal between $16,000 and $32,000 along with drugs and other types of contraband or evidence. In one instance, a police officer stole 1.5 kg (3.3 lb) of cocaine which he then sold to another police officer for $16,000. Initially, raids were intended to enforce laws and to apprehend both the small-time dealers and the major dealers who were more difficult to apprehend. However, over time and due to exposure to large sums of money and drugs, police officers changed their motivations to steal money, drugs, and property rather than turn it in as evidence.

Thefts varied from simple stealing to acts of robbery and murder. Robberies were often committed during off-duty hours. One police officer robbed a liquor store and murdered the owner. In this case, the officer, having ordered the owner to lie on the floor, shot him in the back before stealing the store proceeds (Mollen et al., 1994).

Finally, corrupt police officers became drug dealers and users. The commission determined that there were three ways police officers became involved in the drug trade. Some police officers would become acquaintances with local drug dealers in their areas of responsibility; other officers were able to *fence* their drugs with the assistance of other police officers, and finally, officers would buy drugs from friends or neighbors and then resell them on the streets. As a result of departmental investigations, about 25% of all officer dismissals were for drug use.

The Code of Silence: Cops Don't Tell on Cops

The Knapp Commission formulated a belief that their investigation and findings would permanently damage corruption within the department as well as break the code of silence that protected the many police officers who were ravaging the city through their corruptive behaviors. This was based upon their success in eliciting testimony from corrupt police officers who identified the procedures and participants of corruption, from the patrolmen to the high ranking administrators. While pondering why corruption continued into the 1990s, the answer was found within the report published by Mollen et al. (1994) "Unfortunately, their hope never became reality" (p. 51). Whereas Knapp sought to identify and solve corruption, the Mollen Commission sought to answer the more pressing questions as to why corruption existed in the first place. Their targets were the attitudes and influences that changed the honest police officers into criminals.

The well-known code of silence is perhaps the strongest influence that confronts the police officer. The code of silence simply implies that all police officers will not *snitch* or testify against other police officers due to their fraternal relationships. However, the allegiance to the code is half of the problem. Any police officer who held this allegiance was also seen as supporting and protecting those who were corrupt, therefore condoning this type of behavior (Mollen et al., 1994). Wright (2010) studied the police culture and found a variety of attitudes that were pervasive in misconduct. Reiner theorized that the police culture, in general, was not "monolithic, universal and unchanging." (as cited in Wright, 2010) It experienced change based upon the various attitudes confronting the police officer. Mollen et al. (1994) found that there existed a *loyalty ethic* and insulation that protected the police officers. Due to this, the common attitude of "Us versus Them" existed throughout the department. This division separated the police officers from the community. Wright (2010) found that communal isolation of police officers also resulted in solidarity amongst their own and therefore supported the separatism found by the Mollen Commission. Attitudes were also found during Wright's (2010) study. The attitudes which supported the "Us versus Them" mentality were "...a sense of mission, action, cynicism, pessimism, suspicion, conservatism, isolation, and solidarity" (p. 341). A study by Klockers et al. found that a small number of officers would not report serious or severe cases of misconduct, whereas the majority of officers would not report seemingly minor cases of misconduct (as cited in Wright, 2010). The obvious result of breaking the code of silence was the police officer's ostracization. Such instances would cause *rats* or informing police officers to be transferred between precincts or finding that their reputations had preceded them to their next assignment. One supervisor was assigned to 38 different commands during this tenure with the department (Mollen et al., 1994).

Cynical Attitudes

Police officers are confronted with the realism of crime on a first-hand basis unlike the community's experience with crime. Due to their experiences that can occur almost on a daily basis, police officers tend to become cynical about their jobs and responsibilities. Sobol (2010) explained that police officers are seen as cynical when they experience community members refusing to cooperate with the police, or when the criminal justice system as a whole fails to solve social issues regarding crimes. Cynicism also comes from seeing the arrested suspect released on bail after short durations of incarceration. Further, police officers who suffer from cynicism oftentimes fail to devote their time and energy when encountering suspects in high-crime areas. Mollen et al. (1994) found that cynicism had opposing effects within the department. Those police officers who did not engage in corruption found a reason not to report acts of corruption due to their cynicism that the department would disregard the need for action against corruption, justifying their choice to remain silent on the issue. Conversely, those who did engage in corruption used their cynicism to justify their actions since they saw the department as accepting and condoning corruption. Police officer cynicism remained a doubled-edged sword, which worked against the department in both directions. One major type of corruption fed by cynicism was brutality. Since the criminal justice system in New York City failed to effectively combat crime, police officers saw their own type of justice as justified; crime could only be defeated through the use of the nightstick. If not violent, other police officers resorted to theft or fabricating evidence to defeat criminals. Unfortunately for the department, police officers began seeing themselves as "fools in a hypocritical system" (Mollen et al., 1994, p. 64). Many police officers reported that they believed the system was hypocritical and that policies and procedures were actually rhetoric. One very interesting finding by the Mollen Commission was police cynicism was justified. Many police officers saw their superiors and colleagues engaging in corruption thereby fostering their beliefs that the department and police work in the city were based upon unrealistic expectations. Lastly, it is not what you do but who you know that drives the cynicism in many cases. Promotions and assignments should be based upon merit and successful completion of examinations. However, this sort of favoritism was practiced within the department to reward those who played the game. In short, police officers not treated as favorites were penalized as needed whereas the favored officers were rewarded regardless of their incompetence or misbehaviors.

Character and Morality

In the 1980s, academy classes numbered recruits into the thousands. By the summer of 1994, over 4,000 police recruits were trained and assigned to precincts ready to conduct their law enforcement duties. In July 2013, a class of 1,200 recruits were sworn into duty. Police Commissioner Raymond Kelly reported that this particular recruit class was larger than usual due to concerns of new police officer contrition rates (as cited in NY1 News, 2013). Who are being recruited into the New York Police Department? It is essential that recruit character and morals be determined before hiring and training. The Mollen Commission found that the department oftentimes failed to complete appropriate background checks of police applicants. Of concern were their family experiences, education, and community values. Of course criminal justice checks were required. Considering the lack of proper background checks, the department hired, trained, and assigned new officers to precincts without any knowledge of their abilities to use moral character or psychological prowess to meet the demands of police work in a large city (Mollen et al., 1994). A decline in the quality of recruits was found which had a direct impact upon the department's mission. With the decline in quality recruits came the increase in corruption. Between 1989 and 1994, the department dismissed or suspended over 400 officers due to misconduct and corruption. Another issue noted was the push for more police officers. Absent qualified applicants, politics and community actions pushed for more police officers on the street thereby accepting substandard applicants and creating future problems. Finally, experience, which enhances police officers, could become problematic if the large numbers of police officers are relatively new. Mollen et al. (1994) found 31% of the department possessed an average of 5 years' experience and expected it to climb to 42% with the anticipated addition of four thousand new police officers in 1994.

Fekjær, Petersson, and Thomassen (2014) addressed the issue of police officer character and morals. Their study consisted of two longitudinal surveys of two cohorts of police recruits. A cohort is a group of people who share a common characteristic or experience within a defined period of time. In this case, the researchers followed the police recruits through their training into their assignments for 3 years. The surveys tested the police officers regarding various mundane scenarios and how they would react. The results of the study indicated that new police recruits are more apt to engage in misconduct as they gained experience from their work, the community, or other police officers. Due to the length of the police academy training, recruits typically do not change their attitudes from "doing the right thing" to attitudes supporting misconduct while attending the academy. The typical police officer who changed their attitudes were the young male officers. The question of the effectiveness of recruitment policies and in-service training arose. It was determined that these aspects of police officer development did not hinder "... gradually becoming more positive towards Dirty Harry measures as they gained field experience" (Fekjær et al., 2014, p. 756). For the department, many new police officers were given the power and authority of law enforcement before the age of 23. This new assignment of power, along with the uniform, badge, and gun oftentimes resulted in the young officer's desire of excitement and thrills rather than community service.

See No Evil, Hear No Evil: The Collapse of Control

What failed since the Knapp Commission issued its report in 1972? Recall that the Knapp Commission identified failures within the department's system and made recommendations how to investigate and enforce compliance against corruption (Chapter 4). The Mollen Commission investigation offered a revelation regarding the second major system failure: The New York City Police Department had abandoned almost all efforts to identify and correct the problem of widespread corruption. In short, not much was being done about it. In fact, little historical documentation could be found regarding anti-corruption efforts and the leadership had very little knowledge about how the anticorruption programs were supposed to work. It appeared that since Knapp, the New York Police Department rode the slippery slope into ineffectiveness and despair.

It had been years since the department actively investigated corruption. It was easier to conceal the corruption than to ferret it out and take appropriate action. To this end, the Mollen Commission began a painstaking reinvestigation of the corruption pandemic, once again addressing the primary tenets of anti-corruption efforts: Leadership accountability, investigative efforts, proper recruitment and training, and the attitudes of the police officers. Why did the department allow this to fester and become stagnant? The answer was simple. The department policed itself unlike other municipal agencies. This self-policing and lack of external oversight prevented the city from learning that the department was not doing its part in combating corruption and protecting the city from unscrupulous police officers (Mollen et al., 1994). Greene (2007) opined that the police world is too complex, permitting the police to abuse the system through corruption. Oversight independence and transparency are mandatory since policing has become a sensitive intrusion into citizen's life. If conducted effectively, the oversight process should produce appropriate administration of law by police officers and encourage the community's commitment to the rule of law. The Mollen Commission's theory supported this finding as there was an overall reluctance to find and address corruption since there were no pressures from independent agencies. Some leadership feared the disclosure of corruption since it would threaten the image of the department or damage careers. This belief trickled down to the rank and file police officer who was prone to suggestibility regarding corruption. Official doctrine was present but largely ignored establishing the stance that corruption was acceptable in the department.

This is not to say that corruption was not investigated. Unfortunately, the investigative unit, such as the Internal Affairs Division (IAD), aimed at identifying corruption as infrequently as possible. The administration was not interested in combating serious corruption; they preferred to consider their responsibility as damage control rather than enforcement. One investigator referred to this lack of enforcement as "see no evil, hear no evil." The desired result of this lack of aggressiveness was to prevent bad media reports that the department was intentionally permitting corruption to continue unabated. In 1986, thirteen police officers were investigated and indicted on charges from theft to drug related activities (Mollen et al., 1994). Situations such as these encouraged the department to prevent disclosures of scandals and corruption. It is understandable that police departments would want to conceal corruption in their communities. Community awareness of systemic corruption not only damages the police/community relationships, but police officers through the ranks would face termination as well as low morale within the department. There is another reason why corruption was kept secret by the department. The disclosure of corruption advertised the department's failure to control its officers indicating substandard management. Conversely, nondisclosure of corruption indicated intentional nonenforcement. The bottom line was that the department administration was "damned if it did, and damned if it didn't."

When the Knapp investigation ended, then Commissioner Patrick Murphy instituted a new strategy to combat corruption. Both the Knapp Commission and Commissioner Murphy agreed that a strong centralized investigative program would have positive preventive effects upon the corruption that was pervading the department. This new effort served two purposes: first, the program demonstrated to the community that the department was taking proactive steps to combat corruption, and second, it was expected to discourage the police officers from their misbehaviors. It was essential that the department become more proactive. The question of effectiveness then arose. Was this proactive strategy enough? Centralized control of systemic problems may not reach out far enough to treat the disease of corruption within the department.

Current Surveys about Corruption

Supplementing this centralized investigative program, Mollen et al. (1994) believed that a narrowly defined strategy would fail and that commanders must be held accountable. Accountability must spread throughout the department if any degree of success was to be realized. In a survey conducted by the authors for this text, criminal justice academics were queried about the success of combating corruption. Of the 28 respondents surveyed, 21% believed that enhanced recruit training in ethics would prevent future misconduct. Eighteen percent supported the use of periodic in-service training for active police officers. Only 7% support this in-service training for supervisors, and lastly 54% believed that supervisors were to be held personally accountable for the misdeeds of their police officers.

During these surveys criminal justice academics provided their reactions to the survey questions. One respondent supported the need for holding supervisors accountable for the actions of their police officers. A rationale was offered as:

> They often choose to ignore the bad behavior either because the offender is politically connected to them or is their favorite... If the administration had to face charges for allowing such behavior to continue I believe we would see much less corruption, especially in New Jersey. (Anonymous academic respondent, October 2014)

Another respondent discussed the need for proper training of new officers:

> Training, in and of itself, is often a band aid. Saying that one does "ethics training" is, by itself, incomplete. What exactly is being taught? Is it attempting to address a current issue of unethical practice of decision making? Are we doing blanket training when the problems are specific to a few bad actors? (Anonymous academic respondent, October 2014)

As seen by the Mollen Commission, the attitude of police officers, as well as the administration, is an important indicator of the success of the agency. This attitude separated the police from the community, as explained by another respondent:

> Those of us who have been practitioners, and worn a police uniform, know that this is a most dangerous first indicator of potential major problems. This includes making arrests even if the PC is lacking, falsifying reports, stealing evidence or contraband, using excessive force and basically protecting other officers regardless of their bad conduct. All this adds up to neglecting the fundamental role of serving the community and instead just concentrating on "policing" the community. And in my experience, once this "Us versus Them" mentality starts, it is very difficult to get the genie back in the bottle! (Anonymous academic respondent, October 2014)

Another respondent spoke of the effectiveness of holding supervisors accountable by using critical thinking about the alleged corruption. To this respondent, the importance was the understanding of what was occurring:

> Any accountability process must be able to identify the problem behavior and determine if it was a mistake (not excusing the behavior, but realizing it arose from an actual error and not malice), "incompetence" (officers lacking skills or ability to handle a certain situation – which may be able to be addressed by focused training) and deliberate misconduct—for which no training can be expected to have any positive impact. (Anonymous academic respondent, October 2014)

The same survey was provided to 21 police officers. Of these officers, 48% supported the recruit training in ethics, 19% chose in-service training for officers, 9.5% chose in-service training for supervisors, and 24% believed that supervisors were to be held accountable. Although the choice of proper recruit training was the most common, holding supervisors accountable was also chosen as mostly likely to prevent corruption. It was interesting to note that in-service training for both the police officer and supervisors were deemed less likely to prevent corruption. Also, support for recruit training and supervisor accountability was opposite that of the academics who responded to the survey.

Police officer respondents contributed the following:

> I can say that training in ethics is probably the best answer. Simply stated, training for both supervisors and line officers. Part of the problem in my view is the caliber of applicants entering the profession, exacerbated by age, no real world work experience, lack of maturity, lack of military experience. In the last 20 years, I've seen a steady decline in all of the above. Case in point, we now have two weeks of scenario based training for recruits simply because they have no life experience due to the above cited issues. (Anonymous police officer respondent, October 2014)

Another police officer respondent agreed that the recruit is in danger of becoming corrupt due to suggestibility. This was explained as:

> …. there isn't gonna be any 1 size fits all solution to the ethics "issue," spending extra time with recruits is likely the least effective, simply because once they hit the streets they fall under the influence of FTOs and senior officers and if 1 or more of them are showing the recruit bad stuff then you KNOW the recruit is gonna be compromised. (Anonymous police officer respondent, October 2014)

Commissioner Murphy theorized that holding commanders and supervisors accountable would only succeed if the means were made available to them. This was the impetus of the Field Investigative Affairs Units (FIAU), which was responsible for the investigation of corruption and reporting to the commanders. The FIAUs worked in concert with the IAD. However, the success of these investigative units could only be realized if the police commissioner and other commanders were held responsible. Unfortunately, the accountability of commanders and supervisors waned and this new proactive program failed. The supervisors' commitment to this effort eventually weakened as department priorities changed. By the time the Mollen Commission began its investigation in 1992, the efforts of Commissioner Murphy only existed on paper and the proactivity no longer existed. The question was now, why?

As already stated, the primary reason corruption was so prevalent within the department was the failing diligence and attitudes of those in charge. Those commanders and supervisors who had the responsibility to combat corruption were not evaluated. In fact, they were not evaluated in times of scandal when police officers were discovered committing the various serious types of corruption such as kidnapping or murder. This impunity from oversight permitted their attitudes to become lax and the fear of sanctioning all but disappeared. Even when these supervisors did discover and address corruption, they were not rewarded in any fashion. The most alarming aspect of this was that the supervisors or commanders were aware of the misconduct, and even if their indifference was noted by the administration, nothing was done about it. Here again, the discovery and revelation of corruption worked against the supervisors. As they reported corruption, the department oftentimes viewed the supervisors as poor managers and therefore partially responsible for the problem. Accountability was replaced with discretion; meaning supervisors or commanders preferred that their police officers be discreet about their misconduct.

The situation with the supervisors and commanders was often referred to as "willful blindness" (Mollen et al., 1994, p. 80).

Aside from supervisor evaluations, police officers were also evaluated for their performances. One particular officer, Michael Dowd, who was known for his misconduct, was evaluated by his superior. To demonstrate how these evaluations were misleading, Officer Dowd's supervisor wrote:

> This officer has excellent street knowledge: relates well with this peers and is empathetic to the community. This officer could excel within the New York City Police Department and easily become a role model for others to emulate if he maximized his inner drive to fulfill job responsibilities to the fullest. Must improve attendance and arrest activity. Good career potential. (Mollen et al., 1994, p. 81)

This officer was hardly a role model for new officers since he engaged in many acts of corruption. And due to this corruption, it is doubtful he held any empathy for the community. Perhaps the best statement referenced Officer Dowd's "excellent street knowledge." When queried about this excellent evaluation, Officer Dowd's supervisor acknowledged that he was a discipline problem but was intent on changing his behaviors.

Continuing on with management problems, the commission found that the first level management, that of the sergeants, was failing. This could be an explanation of the excellent performance evaluation of Officer Dowd. The sergeants were poorly managed and in short supply. The responsibilities assigned to the sergeants were too wide spread. The perceived sergeant to officer ratio was one sergeant to 10 officers, but in reality many sergeants were required to manage upwards of 30 police officers. This over burdening of personnel management could prevent sergeants from possessing adequate knowledge about their officers. Workload issues also took a toll upon the sergeants. The commission found that many sergeants were required to respond to *radio calls*. This additional burden upon the sergeants caused it to be "… practically impossible for sergeants to know what their subordinates are doing at any given time" (Mollen et al., 1994, p. 83).

Finally, the integrity control officers (ICO) should be addressed. The ICOs were lieutenants assigned to the task of ensuring that officer integrity was maintained. However, like most other anticorruption programs within the department, this program was a failure as well. The ICOs spent little to no time dealing with corruption since they were primarily busy with general administrative duties. Some of the ICOs reported that they felt they were merely secretaries for the administration. Further, it was suspected that the ICO was intentionally kept unaware of the corruption they were supposed to investigate. In the end, the IAD did not consider the ICO as part of the anticorruption effort within the department.

Research Conducted after Mollen

Upon completion of the Mollen Commission investigation, various researchers conducted examinations of organizational issues and leadership traits within policing and the New York Police Department. Much of the information was gathered from both the Knapp Commission and the Mollen Commission. A question that can be asked is do these descriptions meet the leadership conditions found in both commission investigations? Part of this examination was to identify exactly what a police organization was. As commonly held, police organizations are considered to be militaristic in structure. Officers are armed and trained in the use of deadly force, they wear uniforms to establish uniformity and solidarity, and operate upon procedure and regulations. But this is not the only organization style found. When not acting in the militaristic style, police organizations are also viewed as a work environment and social environment. As will be seen later in this discussion, officers can also be described as social workers, although not officially. This variety of duties can be challenging for the individual officer who is not cross trained in the various responsibilities. Adlam (2002) examined the rationalities found as associated with police organization and leadership. A rationalization is seen as being practical more so than theory or vague ideas. Rational thought is also predicated upon reason and critical thinking and not philosophical theory. Policing requires action (enforcement and investigation) more than philosophical thought. One famous term, the *hunch* is a feeling not based upon facts. It has been used many times when investigators feel they can solve an investigation. The hunch can be viewed as a theory without evidence and is therefore not rational. Since policing is an arm of government there are other rationalities, those being Socio-Political Professional Rationality, Moral Panic Rationality, Critical Emancipatory Rationality, and Socio-Biological Elitist Rationality.

The Socio-Political Professional Rationality is used to "uphold the law, secure social peace, prevent crime, apprehend criminals, prosecute offenders, protect the innocent, deliver on a wide menu of responsibilities and inculcate 'civility' and reasonableness amongst the citizenry" (Adlam, 2002, p. 23). Is this an appropriate descriptor of the New York Police Department during the Knapp and Mollen investigations? Taking the overall definition of this rationality, do all parts describe the department? With the number of corrupt officers, the department did uphold the law, but only to a degree. The officers were responsible for many crimes. Along with this, crime prevention did seem to hold a low priority.

The Moral Panic Rationality takes a different view of policing. In this case, this rationality "... draws its energy from enduring anxieties and fears about the 'human condition'" (Adlam, 2002, p. 24). This means that citizens can develop a perception of the police in general. Depending upon the segment of society in question, this rationality can support the public fear of police due to their criminal and corrupt behaviors, such as violence. Today in 2015, mass demonstrations have occurred due to police use of force resulting in deaths. In this case, moral panic has taken hold of various segments of society. During the Knapp and Mollen investigations, it was found that society was the target of corruption. Recall that Knapp found many citizens providing kickbacks or bribes to police officers, which fostered a fear that the law enforcement element of the city could control the city at whim for their personal gain. In Mollen, narcotics were largely found to target the city through various violent crimes and use of dangerous narcotics. Citizens could no longer trust the police since they were as dangerous as the criminals they associated with. It has been theorized that a society can panic when faith and confidence in the police is lost. If Officer Serpico could be set up by his colleagues and almost murdered, what can happen to the man on the street who intervenes in police related crimes? Consider Adlam's (2002) further explanation:

> "Moral panic" rationality moves into the foreground when it is no longer possible to rely upon police competence in a technical sense or when it is no longer possible to sustain the image of police as fair and just. Miscarriages of justice, abuses of power and the perceived failure of police to live up to the demands of human rights provisions all occasion the subsequent expression of "moral panic" rationality. (p. 24)

The next rationality, which being the Critical Emancipatory Rationality, addresses the need for police oversight. This rationality frees the citizens from undue police pressures or acts of misconduct by reporting their grievances to oversight boards. Of course this does not prevent citizens from lodging false complaints against officers who cited them for violations. Many large police departments have civilian oversight boards as does the New York Police Department. The New York Police Department provides citizens with the ability to make complaints against its officers. The mission, in part states, "It is empowered to receive, investigate, mediate, hear, make findings, and recommend action on complaints against New York City police officers alleging the use of excessive or unnecessary force, abuse of authority, discourtesy, or the use of offensive language" (NYC Civilian Complaint Review Board, 2015, para. 1).

The remaining rationality, Socio-Biological Elitist Rationality, can explain why police organizations have sub-cultures and why certain members of those cultures act inappropriately. Typically this rationality addresses why people seek to become rulers or leaders. This tends to result from their biological heritage and cleverness. However in terms of policing, officers tend to believe that their unique authority over others as stated by law, entitles them to ultimate control over the community. This also supports the notion of discretion; will the officer cite or arrest or will they decide to let the citizen go with just a warning. Adlam (2002) expressed his view of this rationality by stating, "It contains, as a part of its core, the notion that '*we, the police, know best*'" (p. 25).

A relatively recent policing organizational leadership theory is community policing. The theory of community policing is to place the officer into the community on a personal level (on foot rather than in police cars). It is expected that community policing will have a positive effect upon the amount of corruption. Jones and Supinski (2010) found that "officers patrolled neighborhoods on foot and focused their attention on maintaining order. This environment fostered an intimate relationship between the police and the community, who voiced their concerns to local beat cops" (p. 1). An interesting finding was that relationships between police leaders and politicians could result in acts of corruption. Currently, many large police departments conduct community policing if possible. In some instances, areas of jurisdiction may be too large to accommodate this type of program. Further, engaging in community policing requires major reorganizational changes and new programs to plan. It is commonly seen that community policing can be successful with programs like foot and bicycle patrols and community programs such as neighborhood watch. How did community policing have an effect upon the New York Police Department in the past? The Knapp Commission found that the department did not engage in community policing, leaving officers working with little oversight and independence in decision making processes (Knapp, Monserrat, Sprizzo, Thomas, & Vance, 1972). The Mollen Commission found that the department did have a community police effort in place. Police Commissioner William Bratton introduced Compstat (Computer Statistics) in

1994 as a result of the Mollen investigation. Compstat analyzes crime trends within New York City and has produced success in reducing crime. However, this effort to combat crime addresses all technologies whereas it was found that community policing is also successful due to face-to-face communication with the community (Sefer, 2013). As good as community policing may be, both the department administration, officers, and the commission were of the opinion that community policing would provide the opportunity for corruption and not necessarily decrease or prevent its prevalence in the city (Knapp et al., 1972). Those who have researched community policing's success were of the notion that leadership is the key element in the overall success of the police department. This may explain why community policing was viewed as a potential failure during the Knapp Commission investigation. The department's negative approach toward community policing does not agree with research in that appropriate leadership supports policing as a whole, and tends to engage officers with community programs, which might prevent their involvement in corruption (Ford, Weissbein, & Plamondon, 2003).

Earlier it was discussed that potential applicants for the New York Police Department should be screened and background investigations conducted. One example is the 1990 hiring practice in the Washington DC Police Department. In order to adjust and enhance minority programs, which is a praiseworthy effort, the police department relaxed recruitment standards to attract and enlist minority officers. Many of the new recruits were found to have personal integrity issues. Wilson (2012) who researched this issue stated:

> Sources of new recruits might be decreasing because of a decrease in the qualified applicant pool, changing generational preferences in selecting careers, increased competition for persons who might qualify as police officers, expanded skill requirements for police officers, uncompetitive benefits, and many of the organizational characteristics causing attrition. (p. 342)

Currently, the department requires these documents from the applicant: personal history questionnaire; inquiry for conviction of misdemeanor domestic violence; school records; employment records; verification of unemployment; military records; and records check.

Another issue that has been researched for many years is the use of force, and in particular, deadly force. It is important to understand why people engage in deviant behaviors in the first place. Obviously everything is predicated upon learning. One important theorist discussed this in detail reporting that environment is the key to one's behavior whether it is deviant or appropriate. Edwin Sutherland's differential association theory, simply stated, is that people opt to engage in criminal behaviors because there are more reasons to violate the law than there are not to violate the law; meaning that there seems to be more to gain through criminal behavior (this pertains to the gamut of crime) (Perri, 2014). People merely do not decide to commit crimes without some degree of motivation. In fact, criminal behavior is based upon cultural meanings that provide motives, drives, rationalizations, and attitudes. Can this be compared to the New York Police Department? We can view these cultural meanings by stating that the police sub-culture provides the motivation to engage in corruption. The drive to continue this misconduct is the gain that can be realized through the corruptive acts. The rationalization of Socio-Biological Elitist Rationality, provides the idea that officers rise above the community through their unique and abused authority. Finally, attitudes within the department (from administration to officer) fail to properly investigate and prevent corruption. Sutherland stated his philosophies addressing the sociological causation of crime (Wilson, 2012). Sutherland found that criminal behavior was a learned behavior based upon personal interactions with those who indulged in such behaviors. This interaction has been found to be within the intimate range of personal communication, such as in conspiracies. One's learning of criminal behavior is founded upon the normal mechanics of learning.

From these statements it is clear that it applies to criminals in general as well as acts of misconduct and corruption within the department. In regards to the general attitudes of officers, the type of attitude can alter the citizen's view of the police based upon the acts that are committed. In the Knapp and Mollen investigations the "devil may care" attitudes of the officers demonstrated the view that officers were above the citizen and could do what they desired (as viewed in the Socio-Biological Elitist Rationality). Recall how Warren (2011) explained such communications fostered a break down between the officer and the citizen through the interaction between the police and social networks. Citizens often related their experiences wherein perceptions were fostered upon the vicarious experiences of others. Applying the aforementioned to the use of force (which occurred during both the Knapp and Mollen eras), the character of the officer becomes an important part of their actions. The use of force can be committed both lawfully and unlawfully. Smith (2003), while investigating the use of force, determined that force typically stemmed from both physical and verbal encounters with minority groups. Female officers tend to use more strategies in their approaches to volatile situations than their male counterparts. Male officers viewed themselves as enforcers of law and therefore were more prone to use force. Smith's (2003) conclusion was that the presence of women officers had more beneficial impacts on policing efforts.

In line with corruption, the psychology of police officers is of paramount importance. Police departments attempt to find the best qualified applicants for their departments. Most officers are good and honest people who exhibit sound ethics. However, with a large police department such as the New York Police Department, there are many officers who either slipped through the cracks, weren't sufficiently examined for competence, or decided to engage in corruption due to their exposure to peer pressures. Psychology of police officers is a must in the selection process. Fitch (2011) wrote extensively about an officer's psychological experiences in regards to corruption or misconduct. Whenever a person departs from their attitudes and beliefs, it stands to reason that they will experience psychological tensions. This is known as cognizant dissonance; being aware that they forfeited their personal beliefs and ethics for unacceptable behaviors. There are two systems in which officers can excuse their behaviors. One is known as the neutralization theory and the other is rationalizing misconduct. The latter is aimed at police officers whereas the former is used in general circumstances.

Recalling the neutralization theory developed by Sykes and Matza in 1957, the department experienced this defense tactic during the Mollen investigation as well. However this is not the only such theory. Another theory was developed to add elements of how police officers can explain away their wrongful actions. Fitch (2011) constructed a strategy for rationalizing misconduct similar to that discussed by Shoenberger, Heckert, and Heckert (2012). These techniques are listed below:

1. *Denial of victim*: This technique is the same as the earlier since without a victim there can be no misconduct.
2. *Victim of circumstance*: Being a victim of circumstances, an officer would have no choice but to engage in corruption or misconduct. This is due to the pressures exerted upon him by his peers or unethical leadership.
3. *Denial of injury*: As in the neutralization theory, if there is no injury then there are no acts of misconduct or corruption.
4. *Advantageous comparisons*: There are times when minimizing one's actions can be a rationalization. The advantageous comparison can be used to excuse wrongful behavior when others commit more serious infractions.
5. *Higher cause*: The higher cause rationalization is similar to the *noble cause* rationalization. In this instance, an officer may break rules or violate law to remove certain offenders from society based upon their belief that they are doing a greater good for the community.
6. *Blame the victim*: In this instance, a victim will invite their suffering by breaking the law. For example, an officer may use inappropriate force while claiming it was the victim's fault due to his or her criminal behavior.
7. *Dehumanization*: Officers frequently use demeaning or dehumanizing language when referring to their victims. This can be done by calling a person epithets like *dirtbag*. This enables officers to justify and minimize their actions while reducing their personal responsibility for committing inappropriate acts.
8. *Diffusion of responsibility*: Particularly aimed at groups of officers, the diffusion of responsibility permits officers to lessen their responsibility every time an additional officer is added to the group's corrupt acts.

The New York Police Department (2015) employs psychologists for applicants and police officers. The job description reads in part:

> Psychologists evaluate potential candidates for employment for specific job titles (Police Officer, Police Communications Technician, School Safety Agent, etc.). through the use of clinical interviewing and the administration and interpretation of standard group and individual tests of personality development and intellectual capacity. (Careers, para. 5)

The entrance examination for applicants includes two psychological processes, a written psychological examination and an oral examination. For the most part, police departments hold their applicants to a strict psychological examination to determine their fitness for police duty. In some instances, police applicants have been accepted while doing poorly during the psychological examination therefore possibly resulting in acts of misconduct.

References

Adlam, R. (2002). Governmental rationalities in police leadership: An essay exploring some of the "deep structure" in police leadership praxis. *Policing and Society, 12*(1), 15–36.

Bureau of Justice Assistance. (2011). *Plea and charge bargaining.* Retrieved from: https://www.bja.gov/Publications/PleaBargainingResearchSummary.pdf

Carr, P. J., Napolitano, L., & Keating J. (2007). We never call the cops and here is why: A qualitative examination of legal cynicism in three Philadelphia neighborhoods. *Criminology, 45*(2), 445–480. Retrieved from: http://server05/productn/C/CRY/45- 2/CRY2007.txt

Fekjær, S. B., Petersson, O., & Thomassen, G. (2014). From legalist to Dirty Harry: Police recruits' attitudes towards non-legalistic police practice. *European Journal of Criminology, 11*(6), 745–759. doi:10.1177/1477370814525935

Fitch, B. D. (2011). Understanding the psychology of police misconduct. *The Police Chief, 78*(1), 24–27.

Ford, J. K., Weissbein, D. A., & Plamondon K. E. (2003). Distinguishing organizational from strategy commitment: Linking officers' commitment to community policing to job behaviors and satisfaction. *Justice Quarterly, 20*(1), 159–184.

Gilbert, S. V. (2003). *Knowledge area module number 3: Principles of social systems.* Unpublished manuscript, Walden University, Minneapolis, MN.

Greene, J. R. (2007). Make police oversight independent and transparent. *Criminology & Public Policy, 6*(4), 747–754.

Ivković, S. K., & Shelley, T. O. (2010). The code of silence and disciplinary fairness: A comparison of Czech police supervisor and line officer views. *Police: An International Journal of Police Strategies and Management, 33*(3), 548–574. doi: 10.1108/13639511011066908

Jones, C., & Supinski, S. B. (2010). Policing and community relations in the homeland security era. *Journal of Homeland Security and Emergency Management, 7*(1), 1–43.

Knapp, W., Monserrat, J., Sprizzo, J. E., Thomas, F. A., & Vance, C. R. (1972). *Commission to investigate allegations of police corruption and the city's anti-corruption procedures: Commission report*. New York, NY: George Braziller.

Mollen, M., Baer, H., Evans, H., Lankler, R., & Tyler, H. R. (1994). *Commission to investigate allegations of police corruption and the anti-corruption procedures of the police department: Commission report*. New York, NY: The City of New York.

NY1 News. (2013). *NYPD swears class of police academy recruits*. Retrieved from: http://queens.ny1.com/content/news/185281/nypd-swears-in-class-of-police-academy- recruits

NYC Civilian Complaint Review Board. (2015). *About CCRB: Mission and rules*. Retrieved from: http://www.nyc.gov/html/ccrb/html/about/about.shtml

NYPD. (2015). *Application process*. Retrieved from: http://www.nyc.gov/html/nypd/html/careers/application_forms.shtml

Packman, D. (2010). *The CATO's institute national police misconduct reporting project*. Retrieved from: http://www.policemisconduct.net/2010-q2-npmsrp-national-police-misconduct-statistical-report/

Perri, F. S. (2014). Sutherland, Cleckley and beyond: White-collar crime and psychopathy. *Pathological Studies, 6*(4), 71–88.

Rothwell, G. R., & Baldwin, N. J. (2007). Whistle-blowing and the code of silence in police agencies: Policy and structural predictors. *Crime & Delinquency, 53*(4), 605–632. doi: 10.1177/0011128706295048

Sefer, Y. (2013). Tailoring model in reforming police organizations towards community policing. *Journal of Organizational Change Management, 2*(5), 897–924.

Shoenberger, N., Heckert, A., & Heckert, D. (2012). Techniques of neutralization theory and positive deviance. *Deviant Behavior, 33*, 774–791.

Sobol, J. J. (2010). Social ecology and police discretion: The influence of district crime, cynicism, and workload on the vigor of police response. *Journal of Criminal Justice, 38*(4), 481–488. doi: 10.1016/j.jcrimjus.2010.04.017

Smith, B. W. (2003). The impact of police officer diversity on police-caused homicides. *The Policy Studies Journal, 31*(2), 147–162.

Warren, P. Y. (2011). Perceptions of police disrespect during vehicle stops: A race based analysis. *Crime & Criminology, 57*(3), 356–376.

Wilson, J. M. (2012). Articulating the dynamic police staffing challenge. *Policing: An International Journal of Police Strategies & Management, 35*(2), 327–355.

Wright, B. (2010). Civilianising the "blue code"? An examination of attitudes to misconduct in the police extended family. *International Journal of Police Science & Management, 12*(3), 340–356. doi: 10.1037/0003-0066X.59.1.29

4

Judicial Findings and Action Taken by the New York Police Department

For a moment the greatest temptation of my life swept over me. A thousand thoughts of sudden wealth and a life free from the grinding labor which I had always known, came rushing into my mind. Here in my hands were five hundred dollars, or what professed to be, every one of them as good as gold, if I only chose to use it.

Allan Pinkerton (1860), on refusing corruption

Knapp Commission

The years of concern for the Knapp Commission were 1968 through 1972. In an effort to explain and correct the problem of corruption within the New York Police Department, the commission identified various corruption-conducive conditions. Beginning with the overall organization, there were various units responsible for rooting out corruption and other acts of misbehavior. These levels consisted of the following:

1. First Deputy Commissioner's Investigating Unit
2. Police Commissioner's Confidential Investigating Unit
3. Chief Inspector's Investigating Unit
4. Patrol Bureau Inspection Unit
5. Detective Evaluation and Analysis Unit
6. Bureau of Special Services
7. Central Investigations Division
8. Personnel and Administrative Services Bureau
9. Gambling Enforcement Inspection Review Board

Despite having various levels of investigation, the department failed to achieve its goal of finding and correcting systemic corruption. For example, the number and location of the units were many and separate from one another. In other words, there was no distinct organization for the investigating units as a whole. This type of structure lent itself to failure since information was not passed between the needful units. Lack of communication resulted in the misdirection of the unit personnel responsible for investigating corruption. Success for this type of structure required proper coordination so that investigations could be successfully completed. A report issued by the International Association of Chiefs of Police in 1967 recommended that the number of units be reduced to a more centralized command. Therefore, the Inspection Services Bureau (ISB) was instituted under the auspices of the first deputy commissioner. Under the ISB were sub-units designated with particular missions regarding corruption. The Internal Affairs Division (IAD) received and investigated complaints of police officer misconduct to include claims of corruption. Later, resulting from the Mollen Commission investigation, the IAD would take on a more structured role. The Intelligence Division was placed in control of developing and referring intelligence regarding organized crime and acts of corruption by police officers. Finally, the Public Morals Administrative Division monitored the enforcement of vice related crimes such as gambling and other social vices.

As good as this new structure sounded, there were problems with its practice. Initially, the ISB had no authority to investigate or review officer records unless they obtained proper authorization from the chief of detectives or the chief inspector. Without the cooperation of other sections of the department, necessary information could not be obtained, forcing investigators to go elsewhere for evidence. There were times when force was employed to attempt to retrieve needed information from the detective division files. In addition to the lack of authority and cooperation, the ISB also suffered from manpower problems. It was found that a "medium" classified investigation by the ISB could expend between 300 and 1000 man-hours thus occupying an inordinate percentage of the bureau's investigators. The intelligence branch of the ISB was responsible for tracking potential corruptive connections between 30,000 police officers and various criminals throughout the city (Knapp et al., 1972). This initial attempt to better organize and administer anticorruption efforts was on the verge of failure.

Substandard Investigations

The administrative theory about why corruption was present within the New York Police Department was the *rotten apple* theory. This theory states that most members of the organization were law abiding, followed all policies and procedures, and were not involved in corruption. The administration of the department placed the responsibility of corruption upon the rogue police officers who were working on their own while disregarding the department's policies and procedures. It is for this reason many of the internal investigations were substandard in that investigators who believed this theory failed to seek indicators of systemic corruption beyond the single corrupt police officer. Further, investigators approached complaints of corruption one case at a time, meaning that no connections were being made amongst cases that were referred to investigation. This also failed to produce evidence of systemic corruption. Once sufficient evidence was garnered against a suspect police officer, an arrest was made and charges were brought against him therefore closing the investigation. Another issue that adversely affected the investigation was the adage, "we've always done it this way" in that no innovative investigative techniques were explored. It is important for supervisors to review, assess, and assign investigations to the proper investigators or place the investigation in the appropriate file locations. These situations often times resulted in poor management and coordination in the investigations. A question could be presented, "was this indifferent approach to investigations indicative of efforts to protect corrupt police officers?" Along with the lackadaisical approach to the investigations, records were found to be substandard as well. Investigators can be described as historians since they record the history of crimes and those who commit them. Investigations typically require various official forms and records which identify participants, locations, statements, and records of evidence. Minus these documents, investigations can fail and those responsible for crimes can be lost. The department suffered from this failure, in that the file process was severely lacking. Many case files were out of date or had documents missing. No records existed to document where removed records were placed and why. Finally, the police department was slow in updating records systems by installing computers or other modernized record systems. It was deemed that the New York Police Department was behind the times in comparison with other similar agencies.

Systemic Attitudes

Aside from incidents of corruption, the overall attitudes of the department leadership failed to prevent the investigation and prevention of corruption. Returning once again to the rotten apple theory, the administration displayed this attitude in an effort to forego any discovery that the department's corruption was prevalent. Not only was this a method of protecting the department, but it could also protect the jobs of the leadership who had knowledge of the systemic corruption. There was also evidence that police officers had joined the ranks of narcotics offenders, and in one case were suspected of murder. Commission investigators were able to uncover an act of gross nonfeasance in the Narcotics Division. Information, known by high ranking supervisors, was ignored and nothing was ever done about the serious allegations. Upon discovery by the commission, leadership then provided an explanation of why the information was ignored. The explanation was that the information was being "held close" during pending prosecutions. However, others who were allegedly involved in this agreement had no knowledge of its inception. Other similar examples were found by the commission.

Efforts to Improve Shortcomings

The easiest shortcoming to improve was the insufficient manpower. An example of the department's strength could be seen in recruit training. The December 1952 graduating class consisted of 681 graduating recruits. The New York Police Department was able to increase the necessary personnel to investigate corruption. Along with manpower issues, the department then turned its attention to the method in which corruption was being investigated. The theory of investigating corruption was that commanders were responsible. As stated earlier, for commanders to be successful in this they had to change their outlook that the department's corruption was not only the fault of the rogue police officer, and that the rotten apple theory was not accurate. Leadership was the key element in properly changing the behaviors of police officers and fostering a better image for the department. In order for police leaders to be successful, *transformational leadership* should be applied so that appropriate change would occur in the organization. The term *transformational* suggests that the central responsibility of leadership is to foster change (Groves & LaRocca, 2011). Aside from commanders and higher ranking officers, all members of an organization can affect positive change. Those who are in positions of power only are apt to fail in this regard since no positive change is likely. In contrast, *transactional leadership* is similar to bargaining for an end result. For example, supervisors and police officers would meet in agreement regarding expectations where benefits are received. There are two sides to the transactional leadership issue: one is the contingent reward one receives and the other is the management by exception where supervisors take actions only in certain circumstances. With the transformational leader there are three tenets that make these leaders more successful; charisma, intellectual stimulation, and mentoring (Groves & LaRocca, 2011). A study by Orole, Gadar, and Hunter (2014) supported the theory of transformational leadership as being beneficial in preventing corruption. Through the use of surveys to 156 police respondents, it was theorized that transformational leadership had an important and complex effect upon corruption. This study also indicated that while an agency can practice transformational leadership, the perception of corruption will remain. Finally, charisma has a positive influence upon corruption. Can the transformational leader fail by being too personable? It is apparent that those in the New York Police Department command structure who were in positions of power lacked the tenet of transforming change in the department from poor to positive. This was found during the 6-month commander reports wherein no indications of corruption were ever found. A significant change occurred when complaints of corruption were submitted to commanders. The IAD began conducting investigations; however, these were limited to special circumstances such as high ranking officers or sensitive cases. The majority of the complaints were referred to commanders for their internal investigations.

Previously, it was found that many records and reports regarding corruption were either mislaid or missing. To combat this situation, the department set forth the requirement that complaints be thoroughly reviewed and categorized. For example, complaints were to be categorized as full investigation with a report or filing only or filed for informational use only. In addition to this, all determinations were required to be reported within 72 hours of its review. To provide an example of the workload, in 1971, 2,779 complaints were referred to the IAD for investigation. However, many of these complaints could not be substantiated based upon their content. The commission provided such complaints as, "Every cop in Coney Island is a crook," or "There's a black-haired plainclothesman in the Bronx who takes bribes" (Knapp et al., 1972, p. 215). These types of complaints were then dismissed as unsubstantiated. In an effort to conduct appropriate investigations, the IAD did investigate 367 complaints. Of these, 174 complaints were considered not to require any categorization at all.

Finally, the method of investigating corruption was reviewed for possible change. Rather than addressing cases based upon complaints only, the department began an effort of addressing acts of corruption based upon a situation. For example, the seizure of large sums of money from crime scenes or suspects enticed police officers to steal. Understanding this type of situation as overly tempting, the department could take proactive stances to prevent such acts of corruption.

Following the Corruption

What follows the determination of corruption? Sans criminal prosecutions, the police department may take administrative actions against officers who indulge in inappropriate behaviors as well as reward officers for their good performance. The police commissioner, although the highest officer in the department possessing the most authority, does not have unlimited powers for disciplinary actions. As limited as his authority may be, the various options available to the commissioner had not been adequately employed or lacked effectiveness. It was found that the disciplinary process was poorly maintained by inadequate staffing causing a burdensome process.

In order to alleviate this burden, disciplinary options were altered so that minor violations were no longer dealt with by the commissioner. This, however, did not enhance the array of options available to the commissioner.

At some point, the police department may desire to remove a police officer from his official duties as has been seen in today's questionable police officer behaviors. The removal, or firing of a police officer, is considered to be the decertification of that officer due to misconduct. There are two important perceptions involved in decertification; the perception of the department and that of the general public. Police officers must maintain their legitimacy so that policing as a whole and the effectiveness of the officer are not questioned by the community. The public's compliance with police authority is dependent upon this relationship (Atherley & Hickman, 2013). Part of decertification is to permanently remove the officer from law enforcement employment. Losing one's law enforcement certification in New York should prevent the officer from gaining such employment elsewhere in the country. In fact, New York was one of the first states to institute the Police Officer Standards of Training (POST) program in 1959. This training was required pursuant to Chapter 446 of the 1959 Laws. According to the New York State Division of Criminal Justice Services (DCJS) (2014), only appointed police officers may attend the basic police officer training course. The Basic Course for Police Officers began in 1960 with a minimum of 80 training hours. Required hours incrementally increased over time to a minimum of 639 training hours by 2008 (which is still the requirement in 2014). Part of this basic training is 12 hours of ethics which includes scenario-based instruction. Atherley and Hickman (2013) found that an excess of 1,350 law enforcement officers lost their certifications during 2011, which was an estimated ratio of 1.2:1000 police officers.

Levels of Administrative Discipline

Like many organizations, the lesser degree of discipline occurs as administrative discipline. The police department had six degrees of rewards and disciplines. First, the commissioner had the authority to promote captains to higher ranks, namely deputy inspector,

inspector, deputy chief inspector, assistant chief inspector, and chief inspector. Along with this authority the commissioner could also demote these same police officers back to the rank of captain. In the next level and below the higher ranks, it was difficult to reward to some of the mid-level officers (sergeant, lieutenant, and captain) with promotions since these levels were contingent upon taking the civil service examination. In New York City, the open competitive examinations were available for police officers. These examinations were open to the public; therefore, the basic police officer examination was scheduled and advertised for interested parties. The next category of examination was the current and eligible employees. Based upon the examination performance, the mid-level officers could be promoted to the next higher rank. This process was dependent upon the applicant's interest in pursuing the promotion (The Official Website of the City of New York, 2014). The commissioner had the authority to choose any applicant from the three top scores. Conversely, the commissioner, once promoting officers in rank could not demote them. In the detective ranks, the commissioner could appoint and remove any detective at will. The position of detective was not a rank but an appointed status within the police department. In the last two levels, the commissioner could demote any probationary sergeant, lieutenant, or captain, or terminate any probationary patrolman. Appendix B shows the overall judicial actions upon police officers between the years 1968 and 1972.

Unfortunately, these options were not realized against officers and their superiors; an indication that police officers who deserved discipline were protected by the system. The unstable nature of this system enabled others to view how the department was operating with regards to personnel. Knapp et al. (1972) quoted one unidentified commander as stating:

> Sure, there are 32,000 policemen in New York, but all the same the department is really quite small. There are only 500-odd captains-and-up, and we all know, or can easily find out, is each other's reputations and assignments for the last ten years and what's going on in the department not by studying the general orders or temporary operation procedures or the rest of all that paper, but by studying the promotion orders and the assignment orders. (p. 220)

Disciplining Commanders

Like many other positions in the department, high-ranking officers were dismissed, demoted, or relieved of command. It was rare that a high-ranking officer received such actions due to the inappropriate actions of his officers. Also, dereliction of duty on the part of the rank and file police officers did not adversely affect the rise in rank of their supervisors. By 1972, as compared to former administrations, more high-ranking officers were demoted or experienced the loss of their immediate commands. Twenty-five officers in the inspector ranks were demoted or relieved of their commands. This new infusion of high-ranking officers was good for the department in that Commissioner Murphy opted to begin regular rotation of these officers in an effort to combat corruption due to their styles of leadership and attitude of rationalizing the cause of corruption. Depending upon how the commanders led their officers, fewer incidents of corruption were expected. Knies and Leisink (2014) found during their research of leadership behaviors in the policing command structure that leaders who actively participated with subordinates and varied their tasks had significant effects upon their police officers' results.

The Gold Shield

Once appointed to the position of detective the officer can then enjoy the status of this honor as his or her performance requirements are then changed to a more unsupervised manner. Along with this new freedom, the detective was also compensated at a higher rate (see Table 4.1). The New York Police Department did not require a civil service examination for this appointment since it was reserved for the commissioner. Recall that the commissioner also possessed the authority to remove detectives from the Detective Bureau, however this seldom occurred. By 1969 detectives began experiencing reductions in rank. Nine third-grade and

Table 4.1 Departmental Hearing Results for 1971

DISMISSED	DISMISSED[a]	RESIGNED	FILED	PENDING	ACQUITTED	CONVICTED	AMNESTY
30	20	9	6	79	18	56	3

Source: Knapp, W. et al., *Commission to Investigate Allegations of Police Corruption and the City's Anti-Corruption Procedures: Commission Report*, Braziller, New York City, NY, 1972, p. 230.

[a] During this collation by the commission, 30 complaints were dismissed before hearings were conducted. The 20 dismissals were officers dismissed before trials occurred.

three second-grade detectives were demoted to the rank of patrolman. Later by 1971, the relative numbers rose to twenty-eight, seven, and four. The most unfortunate finding by the Knapp Commission was that detective appointments were typically not the result of rewarding superior police work, but rather by knowing those who could make a difference. Detective appointments could also be bought. One police officer informant reported that the going rate for purchasing the detective's rank was $500–$1,000 depending upon the officer's involvement in the appointment scheme. The commission determined that it was believed that the detective's gold shield was for sale. Aside from this, how would a police officer properly be appointed as detective? The process was not static by any means, but police officers could become appointed for a satisfactory record as a plainclothes investigator, particularly in narcotics, or 4 years in the Tactical Patrol Force with an excellent arrest record (no mention of quotas was found). Then there were the other special cases, or as the department described, "… men who had performed well in patrol precincts" (Knapp et al., 1972, p. 224) which appeared to be a catch-all rationalization. Following this era of detective appointments, the department prepared new guidelines for police officers vying for the gold shield. These requirements then demanded: 1 year in a moderately demanding precinct; 2 years in a high-activity precinct, patrol or anti-crime section, and volunteering for the plainclothes enforcement (morals or narcotics). The officer's overall performance was then reviewed for possible appointment.

The Department Review Process

Upon completion of the departmental investigation into misconduct, the police officer then had the right to a review. Charges can be brought upon the officer from several sources, namely the police officer's commander, the Internal Affairs Division, and even the Civilian Complaint Review Board (CCRB). The CCRB was instituted in 1950 at which time the board was part of the New York Police Department and police officers were responsible for investigating all submitted complaints. In 1965, under the leadership of Mayor John Lindsay, the CCRB changed to an unattached organization managed by all non-police personnel. This was done to preclude a perception of partiality or bias by the police department (CCRB, 2014). The CCRB could now prefer charges against police officers. Once charges were preferred, they were submitted to the police department's *Department Advocate's* office for review and recommendations. The process was crafted after normal judicial processes of trial and verdict. However the results, which were not criminal findings, were provided to the department for further action. The findings were not required to meet the *reasonable doubt* standard. Reasonable doubt is defined as the lack of proof needed to convict a person of a crime (Garner, 2014). Beyond that, doubt to a higher degree establishes guilt. Rather, the standard used for the departmental review was *preponderance of the evidence.* This standard does not meet the rigor of reasonable doubt, but is sufficiently convincing to believe that the crime was committed. A good analogy is achieving 51% convincement which is also used during civil litigation since there is no chance of loss of liberty. Following the determination of guilt, the findings were then provided to the commissioner who then made the ultimate decision as to punishments. As organized as this process appears, the commission found issues. These issues were an overburdened process, lack of necessary resources, and delays and a lack of alternatives for punishments. In short, this process was in need of overhauling and refinement.

Departmental hearings were the norm for holding the trial of the police officer. Typically, one person within the department had this responsibility and that was the *Trials Deputy.* Cases which were more demanding were heard by the Trials Deputy as well as two deputy commissioners. It was interesting to find that the Trials Deputy averaged three to four hearings per day in a year's time. An example of the workload for this process was found for 1971. In that year, 1,937 cases were tried, of which 292 were returned to the police officers' commanders for disposition. The remaining cases were sent through the department trial process, of which 186 cases were more serious crimes such as bribery, extortion, larceny and other crimes (Knapp et al., 1972).

Concerning delays in this process, at the beginning of 1971 there were 909 cases pending review; 880 cases remained at the end of the calendar year. One issue was the lack of preparation time for witnesses. During the well-known Officer Frank Serpico case, the delays and the lack of preparation time resulted in his testifying at the hearing without a chance of reviewing his information to refresh his recollection. The issue of undue delay had an interesting effect upon the police officers being tried. The department experienced the *30-day race* when recommending punishments for the officers because they could, at any time, submit their retirement papers and officially retire within 30 days making discipline impossible. If the officer completed his 20-year tenure he was also eligible to receive his pension. This, in effect, was almost a reward for his work and misconduct. Other reasons for delays existed as well. For instance, various motions and hearing tactics would delay the process until past the minimum number of days needed for the officer's retirement date, allowing opportunity to retire with all benefits.

Various disciplinary actions could be taken following trial. However, disciplinary actions were few and lacked variety. The department procedures lacked any choice of disciplinary actions between dismissal from the force or a fine of up to 30 days' pay or vacation time with an attached year of probation time. The commission recommended that a greater variety of disciplinary actions be made available, particularly enhancing the fine of 30 days pay or vacation. It was found that even when fined, the action was taken with a degree of leniency. The punishments for the 56 convictions varied between probation, loss of pay, and loss of vacation time. The average loss of vacation time was 4.8 days.

In the end, the process was subject to a judicial review, similar to that of actual criminal prosecutions. There were a number of reversals following the assignment of discipline, and this was in consideration of an officer's pension being lost following dismissal. Basically, if an officer would lose his or her pension as a result of the administrative process, a reversal was probable as a point of sympathy. The following statement by the commission addressed this situation, "The Department should not be obligated to keep corrupt police officers in its ranks merely because some courts feel that loss of pension is too harsh a penalty for some offenses" (Knapp et al., 1972, p. 230).

Policy Changes to Combat Corruption

Policies and procedures are the rules and regulations that run the organization. They can also be changed to prevent disruptive issues. The New York Police Department Commissioner Murphy made various changes, four of which were made to combat the corruption present in the department. The most significant changes dealt with personal accountability of those in the position to prevent corruption, proactivity to prevent corruption, officer training, and the evaluation of officer performances. It was apparent that accountability was a serious shortcoming in the department due to the attitudes discussed earlier. Officer training, or remedial training if need be, is considered to be continuing education for employees. Although many training programs become repetitive due to the lack of updates, repeating education maintains fresh outlooks on the topic. Currently, the International Association of Chiefs of Police (IACP) has educational programs for police agencies. One program in particular is titled the Ethics Toolkit. This program provides the police officer with the theory and need for ethical behaviors. The IACP (2014) ethics committee has stated, "Ethics remains our greatest training and leadership need today" (Introduction to the Ethics Toolkit). The IACP ethics program has a two-part discussion regarding the need for ethics which is available to all to see regardless of association membership.

The commission provided examples of failed accountability on the part of supervisory officers. One such example was the theft of meat from a meat-packing company by police officers. The supervisor sergeant, who observed this theft, did nothing at the time nor did he report the theft at a later time. Further checking by the commission did not find future reference to this theft. This misconduct was addressed by suspending the officers stealing the property as well as the supervising sergeant; the commanding officer was transferred from his command for the lack of discipline. For a long period of time, supervisors or commanders were not held accountable for the actions of their officers even though policy dictated otherwise. One of the issues regarding the lack of commander accountability was the fraternal atmosphere in the precinct. Can a friend and commander take actions upon those who work for him? It was theorized that not being accountable gave the commanders the opportunity to avoid tensions and other personnel issues rather than face them while actually performing their jobs. Another issue for the police officers was their inability to maintain their responsibility during their tour of duty. Police officers were routinely reassigned from their duty locations. Considering the success of community policing, keeping police officers static in their assignments would enhance their success. There is no globally accepted definition of community policing. Terpstra (2011) discussed one definition of community policing stating that a goal is to "... bridge the distance between the police and citizens, to promote citizen participation, to provide the police with more information, and as a result, to promote the effectiveness of policing strategies" (p. 88). If police officers want to support the notion of community policing, then frequent reassignments may defeat their efforts. Supervising officers, such as sergeants, experienced the same issue as they were frequently reassigned as well. Many lieutenants had no field experience and captains were prone to other administrative duties. The final judgment of the lack of responsibility was that frequent shifting of assignments made it almost impossible for officers and supervisors to maintain some sort of balance in their responsibilities.

Another action taken to enhance supervisory accountabilities was the forming of the Neighborhood Police Team and Lieutenant/Operations Officer Program. The concept of these programs was to place greater responsibility upon the supervisory officers as well as police officers assigned to them. The tiers of command were from the sergeant to the lieutenant and then to the precinct commanders. In this manner, each supervisory officer was held to task for his or her decisions, and for management of those beneath them. The Neighborhood Police Team, similar to that of the community police model, integrated the officers into the local community which gave them a sense of ownership in their sectors. Community policing is not a new concept in law enforcement, however not all police agencies (local, state or county) follow this program. Some jurisdictions are too large to permit effective community interactions. Research conducted by Punch, van der VIjver, and Zoomer (2002), determined that community related policing could actually re-engineer policing in regards to crime. In effect, community policing can be a problem-solver and crime control rhetoric. The department established teams of 20–50 patrolmen with sergeants as supervisors. A senior sergeant was then placed in overall command of the team and was ultimately answerable to the precinct commander. The expectation was that the sergeants were to identify problems within their areas of responsibility and address them by assigning officers to investigate and potentially solve the issues. Maintaining the same officers in the same areas of responsibility would enable the officers to make contacts in the community and build trust with the citizens. The image of the police officer interacting with the community can have a strong impact upon the relationship. Salmi, Voetan, and Keskinen (2000) conducted a survey of 3,271 adults and 986 juveniles (with a mean of 15.5 years of age). The goal of the study was to examine the respondents' opinions of police officers based upon their visibility and presence. The results were interesting since officers who remained within their patrol cars were regarded as invisible and unapproachable whereas officers who were present in the community on foot were seen as approachable and friendly. Salmi et al. (2000) concluded, "Quality of police visibility proved to be an important factor from the point of view of community policing, in which one of the main purposes is to improve the relationship between the police and the public" (p. 433). This same theory was conveyed by the commission who described the potential results as officers no longer being that faceless embodiment. The associated program, Lieutenant/Operations Officer Program, provided the sector sergeants with 24 hour responsibilities under the guidance of the lieutenant operations officer.

On a higher plane, command accountability was also enhanced. It was previously discussed that many captains were regarded as the *fly* captains, or substitutes for other captains as needed. Lieutenants and sergeants were multi-tasking, and commanders were not engaging corruption situations. The enhancement of the command structure eliminated the need for substitute captains, sergeants, and lieutenants who were assigned permanent duties in the precinct, and higher-ranking commanders who were required to report on plans to identify corruption.

By definition, a detective is an investigator who performs with a minimum amount of supervision needed. In order to investigate the wide variety of crimes in the city, detectives were free to roam as needed, and in most cases, make their own flexible hours. Their interactions with offenders oftentimes brought them in contact with potentially corruptive scenarios such as crime scenes and large amounts of property or drugs. With this random lifestyle a detective could be inclined to engage in corruptive actions unknown to his commanders. Generalization of detective work meant that the crimes were varied. To alter this, detectives were then assigned to specialized squads that investigated particular crimes. The separate squads were homicide and assault, robbery, and burglary. These types of assignments removed the randomness of the detective's work and added greater accountability. Specializing in one particular area would improve the quality of the criminal investigations.

In many instances, remedial training is used to correct problems exhibited by police officers. Basic training of recruits should address those issues that have been found to already exist in the department. In a later chapter, ethics training will be discussed in more detail. Based upon the commission's findings it was apparent that such recruit training was inadequate. The content of the training was seen as "skimpy" and even at times as comical in its conveyance to the recruits. Ethics and corruption were part of the basic training; however, the attitude with which it was taught indicated that it was not systemic at all and that it only existed within the personal behaviors of some of the officers, a dismissal shared by the administration. Eventually the department adopted a new attitude in teaching recruits about the potential of corruption. Those who were destined for promotion to sergeant, lieutenant, and captain were also required to undergo academy training in regards to management issues and corruption. Promotable officers to sergeant attended the Basic Management Orientation and the lieutenants and captains attended the Middle Management I and II courses. Training classes aside, the most practical mode of training is field training where ethics are put to the test on a daily basis. Many police officers had been exposed to or participated in corruption during their careers. Finally, after training and application, it was essential that the police officers be evaluated to determine if they did, in fact, learn about the wrongness of corruption and their overall performance. Unfortunately, not all tasks performed by the officers dealt with crimes and because of that, crime and arrest statistics could only measure a portion of their performances.

Mollen Commission

As with the Knapp Commission, failures were found to exist regarding the investigation of police corruption. The commission learned that the investigative elements within the department had deteriorated to such a point that the IAD virtually abandoned its responsibility to ferret out the various acts of misconduct. A primary issue that can be seen in both the Knapp and Mollen eras was the noncompliance of ethical responsibilities. The investigative ethics of the IAD during the Mollen era almost did not exist. Descriptions provided by those investigators who decided to assist the commission included such anecdotal information as "eat donuts and do crossword puzzles," conduct "armchair investigations," and "never leaving the office" (Mollen, Baer, Evans, Lankler, & Tyler, 1994, p. 85). This type of environment would only attract substandard investigators who preferred minor incidents of misconduct rather than more serious acts of corruption. In short, it appears that the investigative arm for corruption was not taken seriously which promoted the sense of criminality amongst the officers. Statistically, the IAD investigated about 5% of the assigned corruption cases per year. With approximately 150 officers assigned to the IAD, only 90 handled corruption cases and maintained the negligible number of 133 cases a year. The burden of the work was assigned to the FIAUs which meant that IAD investigators only conducted an average of two new corruption investigations per year. This referral of investigations from the IADs to the FIAUs resulted in the latter's case load of 95% or more than 2500 cases per year (18 cases per investigator) (Mollen et al., 1994).

When interviewed about the IAD failures, the senior officers reported they were unaware that the IAD was failing in its responsibility to investigate corruption complaints. Between 1981 and 1991, the IAD maintained an average of 5% of corruption cases, however, of this percentage, 30% were minor acts of misconduct, including free pizza, being off post, misuse of department vehicles, avoiding payment of tolls, off duty work as security guards, drinking and sleeping on duty, spending inordinate times in restaurants, and going to the gym on department time (Mollen et al., 1994, p. 87). Other issues found were the closure of investigations before all necessary investigative requirements were completed; a high closure rate of 60% despite the type of minor cases, and inflated and inaccurate reports of investigations. Interestingly, when the Mollen Commission was formed the IAD began to remember its mission.

The IAD supervision of the FIAU units reflected the overall performance of the IAD itself. The IAD was to maintain oversight of the FIAU. In this instance there were two levels of failure; the department's lax oversight of the IAD and the IAD's failed oversight of the FIAU. This domino effect resulted in the collapse of the entire FIAU structure. The IAD was responsible for overseeing and assisting the FIAU units, however the commission found that this responsibility failed due to withholding vital assistance, information, and essential resources. An unwritten policy prevented the Manhattan South FIAU access to the IAD investigative records. The commission cited a case study in which these investigative entities failed to work in concert regarding a large corruption investigation.

Officer Michael Dowd Case Study

Officer Michael Dowd was an example of how corruption and crime could exist with impunity. The case of Officer Michael Dowd is oftentimes used to demonstrate how the New York Police Department failed in its mission to discover corruption and prosecute those responsible. Officer Dowd was assigned to the 75th Precinct. Between the years of 1986 and 1992 sixteen complaints were received concerning his acts of misconduct, as well as other officers from the 75th precinct. These acts of corruption were investigated over a period of 6 years. All investigations were closed as unfounded, or, closed due to insufficient evidence. Even though the evidence against him was strong, Officer Dowd acted with impunity, quite openly, and was widely suspected by others to be corrupt. After all investigations were closed, the department placed the blame upon the Brooklyn North Field Internal Affairs unit which failed to arrest Officer Dowd. During its investigation, the commission reported that commanders intervened during the Officer Dowd investigations since wide spread corruption in the 75th precinct would be quite damaging to the department as a whole. In short, the department was more concerned about public image than it was about routing systemic corruption committed by the likes of Officer Dowd. Lieutenant Lawrence Hotaling recorded his knowledge of the effort to prevent information from becoming public. "What I feel happened was that, whether it was valid or not, it was running through Internal Affairs that the Police Commissioner was not too thrilled with the newspaper articles and everything about the 75 [precinct]" (Mollen et al., 1994, p. exhibit 8, p. 2). Officer Dowd was pursued by FIAU Manhattan South investigator Sergeant

Joseph Trimboli for 5 years. Officer Dowd was found to be one of the most referenced corrupt police officers in the city. Due to the failure of the IAD to provide Sergeant Trimboli with the necessary information to successfully support his suspicions, an FIAU investigation became stagnant. Sergeant Trimboli only learned about this information after the commission began its investigation and conducted private interviews regarding this failed communication. As in other instances, the IAD commanders denied any knowledge of the problem. However, supporting testimony from an anonymous IAD investigator proved nondisclosure was a normal occurrence. This investigator, under the offer of confidentiality stated, "There was no sharing of information between [IAD] and the FIAUs. IAD did not trust the FIAUs at all… [there was] fear of disclosure of confidential information that could be an embarrassment to the department" (Mollen et al., 1994, p. 89). Another question arises, why did the New York Police Department suffer from internal mistrust? One can only speculate that perhaps corruption was protecting corruption. During subsequent investigations regarding the 75th precinct, it was found from informants that Officer Dowd was a member of the Adam Diaz drug gang. In return for providing protection for this gang, Officer Dowd would receive $3000–$4000 a week along with an ounce of cocaine. It appeared that Officer Dowd had a hand in almost everything, including robbery and drug deals. The 75th precinct had a group of 25 officers who were systematically robbing both drug dealers and drug locations, Officer Dowd amongst them.

Concealing Corruption

The commission recognized the New York Police Department for its ability to perform superior law enforcement work. Sadly, the commission also documented their opinion that the department could perform this way in any area of policing except for corruption. This is a disappointing image of the department. The intentional concealment of corruption in itself is a form of corruption. Three methods of concealing were discovered: Minimizing corruption through investigations, concealing corruption through filing and classifications, and other cases not sent to prosecutors or not officially recorded. Each form obviously required intent and in many cases conspiratorial conduct.

Cooperating IAD investigators reported that certain acts of corruption were concealed by minimizing the severity of the case to prevent department embarrassment. This was accomplished by not completing all required investigative tasks or by essentially fragmenting a larger investigation into many smaller acts thereby preventing an understanding of what actually occurred. A question arose about why this occurred. Was this the result of a knowing concealment or was it merely incompetence? Again, the department hierarchy, prior to the commission's mandate, reported that it was the result of a lack or coordination and resources. It was the position of the commission that this rationale could not be used as a catch-all explanation based upon the evidence. To support their finding, the commission offered two case studies, the Officer Michael Dowd/75th Precinct investigation and the Ninth Precinct case.

Officer Michael Dowd had been under investigation by the FIAU for many incidents of corruption. As mentioned previously, Sergeant Joseph Trimboli conducted 5 years' worth of investigations regarding Officer Dowd. It was Sergeant Trimboli's testimony that the commanding officers did their best to protect Officer Dowd from investigative efforts and legal consequences because they preferred to prevent embarrassment. Sergeant Trimboli stated the rationale as, "... did not want this investigation to exist. They wanted it to go away" (Mollen et al., 1994, p. 91). To provide a foundation for this testimony, the commission conducted many interviews which provided sufficient proof that Officer Dowd was being protected by the system. Dozens of IAD and FIAU investigators, supervisors, commanders, prosecutors, and Officer Dowd were interviewed. Thirteen complaints had been lodged against Officer Dowd. To further add evidence of concealing corruption committed by Officer Dowd, no one in the department was able to reveal any acts of corruption during his 10-year tenure as a police officer. Eventually Officer Dowd was arrested, but not by the New York Police Department. It was the Suffolk police who brought him to justice. Had the New York Police Department arrested him others may have been implicated in the corruption and concealment of Officer Dowd's activities. Police Commissioner Raymond Kelly, determined that the failures discovered were evidence that the corruption investigative arm of the department was a failure. Being a significant case of corruption, a commission report was maintained to demonstrate that the commission and department reports were diametrically different.

The Officer Michael Dowd investigation was only one example of concealed corruption. The Ninth Precinct dealt with narcotics. Evidence collected by the commission showed that the top brass in the department ordered that an investigation into the corruption involving narcotics be closed early to prevent the collection of sufficient evidence to identify who in the department was involved in the illicit drug trade. Known as the Allan Brown case, information was developed by the Manhattan South FIAU and district attorney that tended to implicate 15 police officers (including Brown) as being involved in wide spread narcotics activities. An anonymous informant in the department provided information that a group of officers were under the influence of drugs and alcohol while on duty, and stole cash and drugs from dealers only to sell them back later. To prove these allegations, an undercover operation was planned in which a party hosted by Brown was to be infiltrated and drugs seized as evidence. The informant purchased drugs from Brown on three occasions. Unfortunately, after all preparations were made, the investigation was ordered closed 22 days before the party date. Brown was ordered arrested and the details of the investigation were released notifying suspect officers and effectively preventing further investigation of a major drug conspiracy in the department. The commission's final observation was that both the Officer Dowd and Brown cases were examples of minimizing corruption through investigations. These cases were summed up with the following commission statement:

> To argue that the department suddenly decided that they had to dismiss him immediately – twenty-two days before he could lead the Department to a large group of other allegedly corrupt officers – is hardly convincing. If removing one drug-abusing corrupt officer from the job was so important, eliminating over a dozen drug-abusing officers should have been a dozen times more important. (Mollen et al., 1994, p. 95)

The next category of concealment was concealing corruption through filing and classifications. In this case, the department used what was referred to as the *tickler file*. This file was used to prevent reports of corruption from being entered into the system for investigation.

In one instance, the police officer daughter of a senior IAD official was found to be involved in drugs and leaking important information. Due to her father's status, the report was placed into the tickler file to protect her. The following entry was made, "Chief Beatty, Bob, Don't enter this one in any records until later. Assign to whoever you think is best fit to handle it" (Mollen et al., 1994, p. 97).

Later, this case was closed as unsubstantiated without any investigation being conducted. The officer involved was then transferred to the narcotics unit where she continued to make false statements regarding narcotics.

The final category was other cases not sent to prosecutors or not officially recorded. Concealment was based upon the failure to submit reports of corruption to the district attorney as required. The number of cases kept from the district attorney was 230. Other than failing to submit reports, some cases were withheld from investigation by coding. Corruption reports were coded with C numbers. A case designated with a "No C" was considered for information use only since insufficient evidence existed. In this way, chosen corruption cases could be hidden. Finally, corruption cases could be designated as "police impersonation." These reports were sent to non-internal affairs sections where they would be dismissed. IAD handled 1,500 corruption cases in this manner each year.

Cultural Abandonment

In an attempt to explain why the department was experiencing so many incidents of corruption within all ranks, the commission found that the department failed to change the *culture of corruption*. This was seen as a systemic failure of large proportions when the commission reported, "We found a police culture that often tolerates and protects corruption" (Mollen et al., 1994, p. 107). Considering the findings during the commission investigation, it appeared that the New York Police Department had little faith within its organization, the leadership, the command infrastructure, and the police officers. Notwithstanding these failures, there still remained many police officers who did not engage in corruption and performed their duties with integrity. Perhaps the rotten apple theory could help explain corruption after all; rather than having the rogue officers there was a large demoralizing group acting in concert for their personal gain. The commission found that the department became stagnant by not rewarding officers for good performance, punishing officers for criminal activity, and not educating officers as to why it was important to report acts of corruption rather than tolerating it. Recall that the IAD suddenly remembered its mission upon the founding of the commission. Also, during the commission investigation, top managers began soliciting information for use in discovering and punishing those committing corruptive acts; however, this only began when the commission started delving into the managerial failures. The desired character trait of integrity came into the limelight since corruption stems from the lack of integrity. Integrity training suffered during recruit training since both recruits and veteran officers were not exposed to department's commitment to integrity and the mission to combat corruption within the ranks. Further, the police academy relied upon outdated training materials, much of which were from the Knapp era. Following academy training, police officers are required to attend in-service training. The department did not fully enforce this requirement and integrity training was not offered at all. Finally, the department's inaction and knowledgeable ignorance provided the lesson that corruption was not as important as it should have been. The message, in short, was "We don't care."

Corruption Control Reforms

Both the Knapp and Mollen Commissions found that oversight was an essential element of discovering and defeating systemic corruption. There were two types of oversight identified; internal oversight to correct department issues and external oversight which would provide an independent review of the department. It was also found that corruption control should be addressed through prevention along with detection. In as much as detection is important, prevention should be a higher standard since new officers would be exposed to the proper education so that detection would be needed less. Corruption prevention should also include the identification of the causes of corruption and its symptoms. Chapter 5 addresses the current ethics training afforded to new department recruits. In order to accomplish this new reform, the commission found that reform was needed in the areas of police culture and management; command accountability; internal investigations; heightening deterrence and sanctions; and community outreach. In essence, these areas indicate that the department, as a whole, was in need of reform.

Culture and Integrity

Culture and integrity, the first reform, is perhaps the foundation of the corruption problem. For without integrity, corruption will exist. The commission found and reported that the culture and integrity within the department was abysmal for many years. There was a lack of commitment to foster integrity into the officers and the department only opted to discipline corruptive officers if it benefitted the department or certain officers or commanders. Leadership was also seen as a tool to enhance the integrity and proper cultural mores for the department. The proper leadership should begin at the top with the police commissioner and extend down the command structure to the street officer. In effect, there are no bad police departments, just bad leaders. Leaders must convey to the officers and commanders that corruption will not be tolerated in any sense and that appropriate consequences will occur without exception. The commission explained, "It must result in all officers understanding that their loyalty to the Department's integrity must be greater than their loyalty to corrupt colleagues" (Mollen et al., 1994, p. 112). The department is fed through the applications of desirable recruits. It is doubtful that many recruits joined the department with the intent to become corrupt and commit crimes that would provide them with wealth and property. Recruits must be found to be honest and loyal. This can only be determined through the use of the proper and effective screening of recruit applicants. This process must demonstrate to officers that only a select few (in this case the department maintained an average of 33,000 officers) would be accepted into the department and they are expected to meet the rigorous standards set forth by the police academy. Unfortunately the commission learned that this philosophical approach was generally seen as inaccurate and that almost anyone could be hired by the New York Police Department. As uplifting as this recruitment philosophy may be, analysis of the recruitment of applicants revealed that around 20% of officers suspended or dismissed (fired) should never have been accepted as recruits and given their badge and authority to become police officers. Twenty-four percent of these officers were found to possess criminal histories. Poor character was another issue, and in many cases, there were sufficient information collected to substantiate this. For example, one officer was arrested and indicted for three robberies and pled guilty to armed robbery. The officer also explained his motivation for these crimes; it was thrilling and exciting. He eventually was dismissed for theft. This situation, like others, was the result of poor screening. Other recruits also benefitted by lax admission requirements. Some officers had histories of assault, weapons charges, robbery, or narcotics violations. Often times background investigations were incomplete by the time the recruit began the academy. Why were the admission investigations failing? Many of the investigators were more committed to completing the cases and submitting paperwork than conducting in-depth applicant screening. Based upon this information, the commission recommended the following recruitment screening (Mollen et al., 1994):

1. Rise the minimum age to 22 years of age.
2. Requirement of at least a 2-year college degree.
3. The applicant must demonstrate integrity.
4. Polygraph examinations.
5. Random drug testing.
6. Complete background investigation before entering the academy.
7. Require that applicants not be hired based upon criminal history.
8. The revelation of juvenile criminal history.
9. Expand recruitment of military members.
10. Review the applicant's tax records and other financial matters.

But what happens, or should happen after the recruit becomes an 18-month probationary police officer? New officers are assigned to Field Training Officers (FTO) who provide practical training and guidance during the new officer's first year. These observations are the foundation for the new officer's evaluations upon which decisions are made to either retain the officer or dismiss him or her. If this were true for the New York Police Department, then many potentially corruptible officers should have been recognized and prevented from damaging the department's image. What did the department do during this era? Considering the many failures found by the commission, it is no surprise that recruits and probationary officers infrequently experienced dismissal for misconduct with the exception of more flagrant misconduct. This obviously negates the power of the evaluation period. The commission sought to find statistical information to back up their observation and found that out of 314 dismissed or suspended officers, 15% (48) were found to exhibit poorly during their attendance at the academy (Mollen et al., 1994, p. 118). On its face, this sounds serious, but the commission did not further identify what poor performance was. Could it have meant more intensive field training and nothing overly serious that required their dismissal from the academy? The commission recommended that the probationary officer should face a more rigorous evaluation period and periodic screening occur during the officer's career. Finally, which has been mentioned previously, supervisors should assume more accountability for new officers.

Upon successfully applying to the department, being tested for integrity, and properly evaluated, the new police officers are then assigned precincts to begin their full time work. There are 76 precincts available for officer assignment. Some precincts were identified as having more corruption problems than others. Can precinct assignments encourage officers to engage in misconduct? The department's personnel management system had what was coined as the "steady tour/steady partner policy." This meant that officers could work in partnerships or primarily in one precinct for long periods of time. What occurs in these partnerships or tours could potentially influence officers to engage in misconduct. The commission conducted interviews of police officers regarding these policies. It was learned that restrictive partnerships or tours produced cliques which could include acts of corruption. Periodic transfers and change of partners were seen as possible remedies. These transfers would alleviate the tension upon officers who were frequently exposed to drugs and other organized crimes.

Command Accountability

Command accountability, the second reform, identified areas wherein commanders and high administrators could have a strong influence to prevent corruption. The department did maintain command accountability, however in terms of preventing corruption, the department failed. The major remedy was enforcing command accountability regarding corruption. In reality, all members of the department should be held to a high degree of values that would discourage or prevent corruption. It should not be the sole responsibility of the command structure alone. In the end, if needed, the command structure should be the final line of defense in preventing and investigating corruption. If corruption control is not considered a standard operating procedure (SOP) then efforts would most likely fail.

What happens when corruption is found? Who pays the price? Usually leaders or commanders were seen as weak and therefore responsible for failure. Sanctions can be used to combat corruption but the commission did not always see this as fair. Immediate sanctions for uncovering corruption could result in incentives not to report and to conceal the misconduct. To prevent this concealment, it was believed that commanders should be fairly judged and they should receive appropriate rewards or sanctions, not for the corruption, but for their performance in managing anticorruption efforts. Recall that the command structure begins at the sergeant level upwards. Sergeants were seen as the first line of defense since they had one-on-one contact with their assignment officers. Unfortunately, sergeants failed to address acts of corruption by their officers. This failure was due, in part, to their experience and abilities. Officers could test for sergeant immediately after completing the academy which results in inexperienced sergeants. Their average ages were young, and their fraternization with their officers prevented their ability to issue orders. The commission recommended various actions to strengthen supervisors. Some of these actions were a 3-year minimum for promotion to sergeant; an increase of field supervisors during high corruption hours; sergeants should not be assigned multiple precincts at one time; in-service training to include sensitivity awareness for all supervisory officers; and practical management skills for the sergeants academy training.

Internal Investigations

Internal investigations, the third reform, are considered the weapon with which to ferret out acts of misconduct and bring it to the attention of the administration. It can be assumed that any law enforcement investigative agency would have no problem with this mission. However, as mentioned previously, the department opted not to conduct any oversight in this area, allowing acts of corruption to continue unabated. The commission reported that, "… genuine commitment to fighting corruption had virtually disappeared …." (Mollen et al., 1994, p. 136). Internal Affairs, which conducts these investigations, abandoned its mission completely. Had the systemic problem actually been the rotten apple theory, then prevention would have been a key element in fighting corruption. However, since the misconduct began in the hierarchy of the department which took actions to conceal misconduct, sections of the department, like Internal Affairs, no longer had a vested interest in fighting corruption. Due to mounting pressures about the collapse of Internal Affairs, the department began its reformation to change structure and procedures of the office. Former investigations deemed as incompetent were either retired or reassigned to other bureaus of the department. Once regarded as an infected office within the department, changes began to make a difference in its success. With appropriate oversight and scrutiny of the commission, the Internal Affairs office was soon recognized to operate with skill and uncompromising zeal. Again, the presence of the commission was partly responsible for this change.

Internal Affairs has always had the widespread image of investigators who could not *work the streets*, or were inexperienced and incompetent. Many have believed that the investigators wasted time chasing after officers who did not commit acts of misconduct, and their empty efforts would someday earn them a promotion or a choice assignment. Because of the mistrust by the rank and file, Internal Affairs had to reestablish its trustworthiness and credibility with the officers in general. This mistrust often times prevented officers from cooperating and providing them with needed information.

How could Internal Affairs affect these changes? The commission recommended that qualified investigators be hired. These qualified investigators should be compensated for their high quality work. Another recommendation was that Internal Affairs should strengthen the methods in which criminal intelligence is collected. Along with the gathering of criminal intelligence, the investigators had to enhance their recruitment and handling of informants. In the end, all information gathered should be shared with the corruption prevention and analysis unit. Finally, the investigative approach, to include civil rights investigations, is the most important aspect of Internal Affairs. The commission recommended that Internal Affairs revamp their investigative efforts which reflected the standard acceptable investigative procedures.

Sanctions

Sanctions, the fourth reform, advocated the use of frequent and meaningful sanctions against those who indulged in corruption. The commission's warning clearly stated, "The Commission strongly endorses these proposals as sensible measures to insure that legal technicalities do not allow corrupt officers to 'beat the system'" (Mollen et al., 1994, p. 143). The recommended sanctions covered such penalties as delaying pensions and retirement pending investigations; revocation of retirements; allow demotions and salary reductions for sergeants and above; change the statute of limitations from 18 to 36 months for disciplinary proceedings; and financial penalties for officers found guilty in a proceeding. This penalty should be changed to pay suspension for a period up to 1 year, monetary fine up to $25,000, and demotion.

Community Outreach

Community outreach, the fifth reform, encouraged that community policing be made an important part of working with the community rather than against it. Sir Robert Peel, the first chief of the London Metropolitan Police District, began the innovative work of assigning officers to their beats with a mission of working with the community. It was his vision that this new relationship would assist in combating crime and foster the cooperation of the community. It could be expected that community policing would encourage police officers in combating crime as well as corruption. But it was realized that community policing could also increase the chance of corruption for the police officers. The success key for community policing is education for both the public at large and the officer. One of the most important efforts in this regard was the founding and development of the citizens' police academy.

Who Polices the Police?

The Knapp Commission, upon completing their investigation, asked, "Will history repeat itself?" As will be seen in Chapter 5, there have been a number of previous investigations regarding corruption within the New York Police Department. Apparently, the answer to this question is "yes" history will and did repeat itself. As of the foundation of this commission, the collapsed method of anticorruption began to change. Interestingly, this new effort to combat corruption began in the presence of commission investigators. Would this new effort have come about without the commission's presence? The commission also asked a very similar question to one presented during Knapp. What will happen when the commission dissolves and the public no longer expresses an interesting in police corruption? Again, will history repeat itself? There has not been a major commission investigation since the Mollen investigation. However, history will show that corruption within this department revived every 20 years or so consisting of scandal, reform, and backslide. Twenty-two years following the Knapp Commission investigation, Mayor Dinkins formed the Mollen Commission. Now, in 2015, or 21 years later, is history ready to repeat?

In order for the police to police itself, oversight should be available to identify appropriate methods of combating corruption. The challenge was to determine what type of oversight operation should be used. To accomplish this, the commission reviewed and considered various models. Two models were considered but rejected and a third was found to be acceptable (Mollen et al., 1994).

The State Special Prosecutor Model: Rejected

The Knapp Commission formed the special prosecutor's office in 1972. The function of this office was to prosecute, period. There was no responsibility or authority to examine and conduct oversight of the department's corruption controls. The theory used by Knapp to form this office was that prosecutors were the main weapon in destroying police corruption. A major deficiency was prosecutors relying upon assigned police officers to investigate corruption and collect evidence to support prosecution. This obviously formed a conflict of interest, meaning, the special prosecutors were presenting evidence of misconduct collected by members of the organization they are investigating. This deficiency was not hidden from the public. How can the public not see the weakness in prosecutions when officers are acquitted or cleared of misconduct when the evidence comes from other officers? The good news is that local and federal prosecutors were welcoming the opportunities to investigate and prosecute corrupt police officers. In 1990, the special prosecutor's office was disbanded which resulted in district attorneys funding and supporting corruption investigations. As shown previously, the presence of the commission had some degree of influence in these changes. Prosecutions did increase upon the establishment of the commission. Even though prosecutors were welcoming of referrals, the commission did feel that a method of continuing the interest of prosecutors in the investigation of corruption should be established. Reestablishing the special prosecutor's office was not recommended since it would do little to combat corruption and their mission would still be prosecutory only. Corruption control was needed to penetrate all levels of the department. The commission's opinion was, "Quality prosecutions will do little to improve commitment, recruitment, screening, training, supervision, accountability, and all the many other necessary ingredients of successful corruption control" (Mollen et al., 1994, p. 151).

Inspector General Model: Rejected

Many government entities relied upon the inspector general model to investigate improprieties. Some opinions focused upon using the inspector general model rather than the internal affairs units; this never came about since evidence demonstrated that the various anticorruption units failed in their responsibilities to ferret out corruption. The inspector general unit is typically an external, impartial, and unbiased entity free of undue influence. External oversight has been shown to provide evidence which is not influenced by the entity under investigation. The support to appoint an inspector general office was founded in the wide belief that the department was unable and unwilling to carry on anticorruption functions. In light of this information, the inspector general model seemed to be the best choice. However, the commission rejected this model since it removed all authority from the department to investigate itself. The commission supported the idea that the commission maintain this responsibility since no other agency in the city was able to make important decisions about the police department. In fact, the New York City department of investigations was relied upon to investigate all city agencies in regards to corruption; all except the New York Police Department. In saying this, the commission believed that the department was able to police itself. In order to show that the department can succeed in this venture, the commission sought to develop and enforce some method that would compel the department to conduct proper anticorruption investigations.

Proposed Oversight Model

In an effort to provide an answer to the failures of investigating corruption, the Mollen Commission used two important principles that were formed during the investigation of the department's efforts to discover and decrease corruption. These principles, independent oversight, and command accountability, if used correctly could strengthen the removal of corruption from the department and hopefully discourage officers from engaging in future acts of corruption. Recall that independent oversight hopefully provides impartial and unbiased examinations of misconduct. Much like the Knapp and Mollen commissions, improvements can be expected to occur within a reasonable time frame as it occurred in the 30th Precinct when the commission was present during corruption investigations. Command accountability places the onus upon the leaders of the department which has been lacking. Holding one accountable for systemic failures can be expected to pressure the responsible leaders to prevent their own career demise. Conceptually, this sounds like an excellent idea. But who will be responsible for enforcing these principles? The commission did state that the department should not lose their responsibility in combating corruption. Who will provide the independent oversight?

The recommendation was that once the commission disbanded, an independent oversight entity should exist. Command accountability would include a total revamping of the present anticorruption program. This revamping, to be successful, would reach deeply into the department since combating corruption was everyone's responsibility.

Command accountability would require the strengthening of all anti-corruption programs through the improvement of seeking quality recruits, updated training, command and supervision, corruption prevention, internal investigations, enforcement of command accountability, and finding and eradicating the roots of misconduct. The newly formed oversight commission would work hand-in-hand with the department.

The creation of the oversight entity would be in the form of a police commission, externally independent from the department. The commission listed four goals for this newly formed commission. The first goal, which is the most obvious, was the continual assessment and audit of all anticorruption efforts. This could be accomplished after all necessary documents and reports are made available to the police commission. Once command accountability has been enhanced, the sharing of information would assist in this part of the police commission's efforts. The second goal addressed the new policies and programs that would be needed to improve anticorruption efforts. It was the hope that adequate policies and programs would affect a change of the misguided values that resulted in misconduct. The police commission members would be responsible for assisting the department in crafting these policies and programs. The third goal, although rather vague, called for the enhanced and successful command accountability to guide the department. The fourth and final goal provided the police commission the ability to begin its own investigations if deemed necessary. Since the police commission was to be an external entity, it was to be regarded as a tool for the police commissioner and mayor as they perceived the success and failures of the department. The commission also described the police commission as "the watchdog for the public" (Mollen et al., 1994, p. 153).

The commission then documented its rationales for structuring the police commission program. The police commission clearly needed the ability to conduct their own independent investigations to assess the control of corruption and to gather needed intelligence to support such investigations. One type of investigative effort was the application of integrity tests. Simply put, an integrity test for police officers can involve setting up an officer to observe their reactions to potentially corruptive behaviors. Rothlein (2010) in *Conducting Integrity Tests on Police Officers*, provided clarity concerning the use of integrity tests. Integrity tests are used in many states. However, not all tests use the same standards. For example, most states prefer to use what is known as the "subjective test," which assesses the officer's state of mind. The fear is that an officer may be entrapped into performing a behavior that indicates he would be a potential corruption risk. As generally known, entrapment is an act perpetrated by the government or agent of the government that may tend to induce a person into committing a criminal act while the person is not predisposed to do so. Persons known to be predisposed to commit such acts cannot be entrapped. The second test is the *objective test,* which assesses the amount of governmental involvement which tends to force the officer into committing potential criminal acts. This test does not require state of mind. Unfortunately, conducting integrity tests for the New York Police Department may become burdensome. Rothlein (2010) explained that, "Targeting police officers who are engaging in criminal misconduct and have been trained in investigative techniques is a difficult process from the onset" (p. 1, para. 16). Since the members of the police commission are not officers, the department would be responsible for this type of investigation. The commission did note that their presence and assessment of the department did produce action on the part of the department. In order to explain this comment further, the commission reported, "Without such a [investigative] capacity, we believe it unlikely that the department would have responded to the Commission's evidence – or attempted to generate its own – as quickly or aggressively as it did" (Mollen et al., 1994, p. 153).

An interesting condition for membership in the police commission was the appointment of five "reputable and knowledgeable citizens," who would agree to work pro bono, or for no compensation. This part of the membership condition was in deference to the fiscal condition of the city's budgetary ailments. These appointments were to be conducted under term limitations to preclude limited decisions as well as preventing inappropriate relationships with the department's bureaucracy that could compromise the commission's independence. During this discussion, the commission did not define "knowledgeable citizens." Since the police commission was staffed by nonlaw enforcement personnel, it is unlikely they were knowledgeable about police operations and corruption prevention. This term remained undefined in the commission's report.

As stated, the organization of the police commission would reflect the same structure as the Mollen Commission possessed. Approximately 10–15 staff members would represent attorneys, investigators, police management experts, and analysts. Further coordination could be made by the police commission with other agencies on an as-needed basis. The primary focus of the police commission would be to review and monitor the anticorruption efforts of the department, monitor cultural conditions, and monitor corruption trends.

Recognizing that many officers did not engage in corruption, these honest police officers were said to experience "quiet pain" as described by Lieutenant Robert McKenna as he testified in public hearings:

> But you know what really hurts? It's when he [the honest officer] goes to pick up his kids from school. Because parents talk, kids listen; they're at school, they talk among themselves. A little kid comes in, he sits in the back seat. He's got bright eyes and he looks at his Daddy. He says, "Daddy, do you steal money?" The cop's stomach tightens. Some cops cry silently. Others just wish it was a bad dream, and it'll go away. (Mollen et al., 1994, p. 158)

References

Atherley, L. T., & Hickman, M. J. (2013). Officer decertification and the national decertification index. *Police Quarterly, 16*(4), 420–437. doi: 10.1177/1098611113489889

Garner, B. (2014). *Black's law dictionary* (10th ed.). Boston, MA: Thomson. Retrieved from: http://thelawdictionary.org/reasonable-doubt/

Groves, K. S., & LaRocca, M. A. (2011). An empirical study of leadership ethical values, transformational and transactional leadership, the follower attitudes toward corporate social responsibility. *Journal of Business Ethics, 103*, 511–528. doi: 10.1007/s10551-011-0877-y

International Association of Chiefs of Police. (2014). *Introduction to the ethics toolkit.* Retrieved from: http://www.theiacp.org/Introduction-to-the-Ethics-Toolkit

Knapp, W., Monserrat, J., Sprizzo, J. E., Thomas, F. A., & Vance, C. R. (1972). *Commission to investigate allegations of police corruption and the city's anti-corruption procedures: Commission report.* New York, NY: Braziller.

Knies, E., & Leisink, P. (2014). Leadership behavior in public organizations: A study of supervisory support by police and medical center middle managers. *Review of Public Personnel Administration, 34*(2), 108–127. doi: 10.1177/0734371X13510851

Mollen, M., Baer, H., Evans, H., Lankler, R., & Tyler, H. R. (1994). *Commission to investigate allegations of police corruption and the anti-corruption procedures of the police department: Commission report.* New York, NY: The City of New York.

New York State Division of Criminal Justice Services. (2014). *Basic course for police officers.* Retrieved from: http://www.criminaljustice.ny.gov/ops/training/bcpo/bcpo01.htm

NYC. Civilian Complaint Review Board. (2014). Retrieved from: http://www.nyc.gov/html/ccrb/html/contact/contact.shtml

Orole, F. A., Gadar, K. B., & Hunter, M. (2014). Leadership style, policing and perception of corruption: A comparative preliminary study within the Nigerian police force. *Psychosociological Issues in Human Resource Management, 2*(2), 79–93.

Punch, M., van der Vijver, K., & Zoomer, O. (2002). Dutch "COP": Developing community policing in the Netherlands. *Policing: An International Journal of Police Strategies and Management, 25*(1), 60–79. doi: 10.1108/1363951020417908

Rothlein, S. (2010). *Conducting integrity tests on law enforcement officers.* Retrieved from: http://www.llrmi.com/articles/legal_update/le_integrity_tests.shtml

Salmi, S., Voeten, M. J. M., & Keskinen, E. (2000). Relation between police image and police visibility. *Journal of Community & Applied Social Psychology, 10*, 433–447. doi: 10.1002/1099-1298(200011/12)10:6<433::AID-CASP576>3.0.CO;2-Z

Terpstra, J. (2011). Governance and accountability in community policing. *Crime Law Social Change, 55*, 87–104. doi: 10.1007/s10611-011-9271-y

The Official Website of the City of New York. (2014). *Civil Service exam information.* Retrieved from: http://www1.nyc.gov/nyc-resources/service/2862/civil-service-exam-information

5
Training Ethics for the Police Recruit

> I hereby acknowledge that I am aware that as a New York City Police Officer there are certain standards of conduct to which I must adhere, both on and off duty. I also acknowledge that I have been reminded about specific conduct, as listed below, that is prohibited and which I should be aware of. I know that this list is not at all inclusive but is only meant to reinforce other training and to help me succeed as a probationary police officer.
>
> **NYPD Acknowledgment of Responsibilities**

Police officer training was a recurring theme throughout the commission investigations examined for this discussion. Due to the unique responsibilities placed upon officers, some of which may result in someone's death, training is essential both by the academy for initial training, and then throughout an officer's career during in-service training. It is understandable that new recruits are trained in the necessary skill sets of which they had no prior knowledge or experience. However, all police officers should engage in the various in-service opportunities afforded to them. But should they engage in training regarding all their skills or should they seek to learn about new technologies instead? Records, reports, and operational data were automated in the early 1980s when computers began to appear on a large scale. Since technology continues to evolve, the police officer on the street should be expected to evolve with it. In January 2015, $160,000,000 in forfeitures (law enforcement agencies that seize property or money during investigations may use the benefit of the *forfeiture*) was earmarked for upgrading the New York Police Department's mobile communications (Weiss, 2014). This new effort would place Smart phones in the hands of approximately 35,000 officers as well as install *ruggedized* computers into 6000 patrol cars. Since many of the 35,000 officers may not have experience with these new technologies, they will undoubtedly attend in-service training classes. In-service training is a mandatory function of enhancing an officer's abilities and knowledge base. Along with new technologies, case law continues to add more legal aspects of criminal justice that officers need to understand to efficiently do their jobs. But can the system really *teach old dogs new tricks*? Etter and Griffin (2011) found that police officers must receive in-service training because "... laws change, technology and equipment improves, the demographics of the population change" (p. 234). In their research, Etter and Griffin (2011) examined an andragogical approach (adult instruction focusing more on the process rather than the content) to explain in-service training for older police officers. They found that many older officers need in-service training but in a more andragogical sense. They also found that older officers had completed 20 years of service or were 40 years old. The age span of older officers is from 40 to 65 years. In the United States, an estimated 262,117 officers are older than 40 years. They were also found to be comfortable within their police subculture, rather cynical, and perhaps resentful of change. The more common categories of police in-service training involve *mandatory training*, *operational training*, and *career-oriented training*. Before discussing the New York Police Department basic recruit training, it is important to state exactly what ethics and values are.

Defining Ethics

According to Merriam-Webster (2014), ethics is described as "rules of behavior based on ideas about what is morally good and bad" (para. 1). The inclusion of the term "morally" is often confusing as this word may be used interchangeably during conversation. *Morals* refers to following the principles of right and wrong (Pollock, 2014, p. 6), whereas ethics involves a broader exploration into defining morals. The importance of understanding ethics comes with the application of established standards of behavior. Within the criminal justice profession, this translates to behaviors that impact others and relate directly to the criminal justice professional. Many professions have their own litany of ethical expectations. The ethics within policing hinges upon the authority and power the officers possess. For example, officers have the ability to use discretion when confronting citizens regarding their misconduct. A very common situation is the everyday traffic stop wherein the officer can decide not to cite the driver. In some states, such as California, speeding enforcement is rather limited in that officers may cite, should cite, or will cite based on the degree of the violation. Officer discretion provides the ability to judge others; therefore, the giving of gifts (free meals or other gratuities) after the fact can constitute a consideration between the officer and citizens. An interesting analogy can be found here; if an officer establishes a consideration with a business owner valued approximately $20, is that the officer's price to be bought? Due to this type of situation, it is no wonder that many believe that the acceptance of gifts by police officers is acceptable. After all, a patrol car parked in front of a business certainly provides a degree of security and comfort to the business owner. Conversely, since many drivers have no way to provide a gift or gratuity, the opposite can be accepted as well that providing gratuities to police officers is wrong.

Pollock (2014) adds examples of ethical formulism and utilitarian ethics to police ethics. The first principle of ethical formulism finds that there should be a blanket degree of comfort providing police officers with gratuities from all business owners. This would most likely be found as unacceptable by the community. The second principle of ethical formulism states that each person is to be treated as an individual and not as a means to an end. In the police situation, where a business owner provides gratuities to officers in return for parking considerations, the action is clearly wrong since the officer is being treated as the means to the end (parking consideration).Gratuities may be held as acceptable under the utilitarian ethics if there were "no strings attached," however what about the mere appearance of improprieties or considerations?

Appendix C contains the Police Code of Ethics, which is ascribed to by the New York Police Department (2014, p. 2). This code is also generally ascribed to by other police agencies as well. The International Association of Chiefs of Police (n.d.) has an honor code also addressing police officer integrity:

> On my honor, I will never betray my badge, my integrity, my character or public trust. I will always have the courage to hold myself and others accountable for our actions. I will always uphold the constitution, my community and the agency I serve. (Oath of Honor)

Making ethical decisions seems easy since most people do not think about applying the theory of ethics as it relates to their everyday lives. Ruggiero (as cited in Pollock, 2014) suggested that in order to make ethical decisions, the dilemma should be evaluated using three criteria. The first criterion is to self-evaluate one's duties upon agreeing to fulfill obligations due to promises or agreements. In policing, this could mean that anti-corruption duties are paramount when deciding to investigate complaints of corruption. The next criterion requires an examination of one's moral ideas as they relate to prudence, temperance, justice, honesty, and compassion. In the case of corruption investigation, one would consider their morality in justice and honesty in reporting the corruption. Finally, the last criterion is to evaluate the intended act to determine if it would have good consequences (utilitarian ethics is for the greater good). In the corruption investigation, discovering and preventing corruption is for the greater good of the community. Close and Meier (as cited in Pollock, 2014) used questions to evaluate a potential unethical act:

1. Does the action violate another person's constitutional rights, including the right of due process?
2. Does the action involve treating another person only as a means to an end?
3. Is the action illegal?
4. Do you predict that your action will produce more bad than good for all persons affected?
5. Does the action violate department procedure or professional duty? (p. 41)

A simple test offered by Pollock (2014) is called the "front page" test. This test asks if you would be happy if your decision were to appear on the front page of the newspaper. A final interesting type of ethics is situational ethics. Simply put, situational ethics states that different situations require different types of responses; therefore, an action can be deemed right or wrong depending on the circumstances of the situation.

What Are Values?

Values are personal in nature, with importance placed by priority for the individual. Values constitute ethical decision making with focused relevance for the criminal justice professional. Some values within the ethical system for these professionals, as shared by Pollock (2014), include "privacy, freedom, public order, justice, duty, and loyalty" (p. 10). These are typical elements of ethical decision making that stem from making judgments based on perceived worth. However personal these values may be, researchers have alternative explanations regarding how police officers use their values at work. Walker and Kratcoski (1985) examined police values in a cross-cultural perspective as it applied to community relations. They opined that the police officer was the key to improving the relationship between the police department and the community, particularly with minority groups within major cities. Two theories were used to explain the values of police officers. Radelet (as cited in Walker & Kratcoski, 1985) stated that how police officers saw themselves resulted from a number of personal influences. Of these personal influences, there are early socialization and occupational socialization. There is no guarantee that a person can develop values in their early life to match the needs of the community and police department. Walker and Kratcoski (1985) coined two theories based on Radelet's ideas of socialization. The *recruitment theory* holds that those entering policing have different traits than the people in the community in which they will practice law enforcement. Some authorities see this as the basis for an authoritarian personality, which is common in many police officers. This can result in further clashes between the police and minority communities. The second theory, the *socialization theory*, holds that police officers will reflect the values of the community. The eventual development of the authoritarian trait adversely affects this as the officer develops cynicism and punitive beliefs from their job.

The New York Police Department has established the following departmental values:

1. Protect the lives and property of our fellow citizens and impartially enforce the law.
2. Fight crime, both by preventing it and aggressively pursuing violators of the law.
3. Maintain a higher standard of integrity than is generally expected of others because so much is expected of us.
4. Value human life, respect the dignity of each individual, and render our services with courtesy and civility.

Professional Ethics

In service professions, established codes of ethics guide behaviors in similar ways. The New York City Fire Department publishes its mission statement and core values on its website. The framework for firefighters differs from the New York Police Department with service, bravery, safety, honor, dedication, and preparedness as key elements (FDNY, 2014). The American Nurses Association includes compassion and respect in the standards of ethical care (ANA, 2014). These three service professions present similar ethical frameworks through the published descriptions of their core concepts, weaving ethical considerations and decision making through common elements of trust, respect, safety, and community.

Teaching Ethics to Police Students

Basic police recruit academy training includes the main document regarding ethics, which is called *Police Studies: Policing with Integrity*. This section of the academy training provides the lessons taught to recruits in an effort to assist in understanding corruption and how it can be fought. Logically, this portion of their training begins with the history of corruption suffered by the department. One cannot learn to appreciate the importance of the topic unless the seriousness is provided. As with historic events, memories tend to fade leaving only the more recent events in the mind of the community. The main corruption events occurred in 1890, 1912, 1930, 1949, 1970, and 1994. During the Mollen investigation, it was found that systemic corruption occurred approximately every 20 years; to be exact, history shows that the average time between these events was 20.8 years. This repetitiveness indicates that, regardless of the efforts of the department and New York City, efforts to identify and stop corruption failed. As of 2014, 20 years have passed without a major investigation of systemic corruption; is it due to reappear? The New York Police Department was established in 1845 and met its first corruption challenge 45 years later.

Lexow Investigation

In the early days of 1890s, New York City was rife with prostitution, gambling, and other forms of vice. In fact, the sex trade was not finally removed from 42nd Street in Manhattan until 1996. Sweeping changes did not come about until the community's uproar forced the government to investigate and take action. Accusations were made that both government officials and the police were involved in corruption as well as being complicit in other illegal acts. As it occurred during the Knapp investigation many years later, local news reporters investigated these claims, which led the city to appoint Senator Charles Lexow to head a committee regarding city corruption. This committee then interviewed more than 500 witnesses and concluded that police officers were, in fact, involved in acts of corruption including bribes, prostitution, con games, brutality, and extortion. Suspicions were that the investigation was motivated by politics. Aside from politics, many police officers faced legal actions against them; however, no convictions or dismissals were successful upon appeal. Theodore Roosevelt, then the president of the Board of Police Commissioners, replaced senior officers for their noncompliance of local laws. His efforts to begin combating corruption were to heighten the standards of discipline and begin a more stringent approach to enforce vice laws.

Curran Committee

The Curran Committee surrounded the death of one Herman Rosenthal. On July 16, 1912, Rosenthal was murdered on 43rd Street, which is located in Times Square, New York City. Even though the murder was witnessed by the police, no arrest was made; essentially the police at the scene ignored the murder completely. Again local media reported on the murder and found that Rosenthal was an informant for the district attorney and was pending his appearance before a grand jury. Rosenthal was a casino owner and had paid Lieutenant Charles Becker for protection. Becker, the commander of a *strong arm squad*, was indicted and convicted of murdering Rosenthal and was subsequently executed along with four others.

Following implications that police officers were involved in corruption (extortion by Becker), the Curran Committee was appointed to investigate the police department. Their investigation revealed that the police department was involved in the extortion of gamblers and brothels, took bribes to *throw cases*, and overall condoning the lax discipline in the department.

Seabury Investigation

August 1930, Court of Appeals Judge Samuel Seabury was appointed to once again conduct an investigation of the police department regarding acts of corruption. The focus of this investigative effort was lawyers, bondsmen, political brokers, the police, and courts. The uncovered scam revealed that bribery and extortion were widely occurring, where police officers and prosecutors were accepting bribes to throw cases in court. Bondsmen were accepting bribes so the arrested could obtain release from jail. Any person who was extorted by this system and did not pay was guaranteed a conviction in court by participating judges. Results from this scam showed that police officers were found to be in possession of inordinate amounts of money, a prostitute pending her testimony was murdered, and a judge disappeared forever. This judge was identified as Judge Joseph Crater who hailed a taxi and was never heard from again. This event has been celebrated as the most "missingest man in New York."

Gross Investigation

In 1949, Julius Helfand was appointed to conduct an investigation concerning local students being victimized by bookmakers. Helfand was the assistant to Kings County District Attorney Miles McDonald. Helfand's efforts identified Harry Gross who worked as a Brooklyn bookmaker, reportedly paying $1,000,000 a year to gain police protection for his illegal operation. Upon his arrest and pending prosecution, Gross agreed to plead guilty to his gambling enterprise and provided information to Helfand. Gross identified 21 police officers who were ultimately charged with conspiracy for taking bribes to not enforce local laws that would impede Gross's actions. Beyond the initial 21 officers, 60 other officers were named as unindicted co-conspirators (these officers were in the ranks of patrolman to assistant chief inspector). At the time of trial, Gross refused to testify, which led to the dismissal of the charges on the 21 officers due to insufficient evidence. Another issue that was uncovered during Helfand's investigation was the existence of *stand ins*, or those who have not committed any crimes and were paid to *take the rap* by bookmakers. The remaining events from 1970 and 1994 were both the Knapp and Mollen investigations, which were discussed previously.

New Organization Affecting Officer Ethics

Police recruits are engaged in education of the department reorganization. Since the last major corruption investigation was conducted by the Mollen Commission, the new organization of the department was predicated upon their findings. Recall that the charges made by the *New York Post* in 1992 began the need for the Mollen investigation of the department. By 1993 the department issued Interim Order 1 (Mollen et al., 1994). This interim order was entitled Establishment of Internal Affairs Bureau. This new effort to investigate corruption resulted in the end of the Inspectional Services Bureau and caused the reorganization of the department's investigation efforts. As shown previously, the investigative functions within the department were eventually found to be a failure in many respects. The Internal Affairs Bureau was originally founded during the Knapp era in 1972. Throughout the Knapp and Mollen eras, the Internal Affairs Bureau was found to be ineffectual, which resulted in the increase of incorruption, where officers engaged in more criminal and heinous acts. In a current view, aside from being the investigator of corruption, the Internal Affairs Bureau has other characteristics as well. In one respect, the Internal Affairs Bureau is considered to be the protector of the department's overall reputation. Throughout recent history, various incidents have occurred where officers have committed violent acts that brought criticism upon officers in general. One of the more publically scrutinized events was the assault of Abner Louima. Upon responding to a fight, officers arrested Louima based on questionable information. The officers then beat Louima with their fists, nightsticks, and hand-held radios while transporting him to the local precinct.

After arriving at the precinct, the beatings continued during which Louima was sexually assaulted with a broomstick. Following the assault, one of the officers then bragged about the beating to others. This event brought discredit upon the department as a whole. It is typical that detractors of the department would generalize the events and place the blame upon the department officers as a whole. Another characteristic placed upon the Internal Affairs Bureau describes its "unparalleled integrity." The new characteristic has demonstratively changed between 1972 and the current administration in 2015 as evidenced by the restructuring of the Internal Affairs Bureau. Is it possible that the once corrupted bureau has changed to a pristine bureau? The remaining characteristic states that the Internal Affairs Bureau is "...thoroughly and effectively intolerant of corruption throughout the department" (New York Police Department, 2014, p. 10).

In view of these new characteristics of the Internal Affairs Bureau, new recruits require knowledge of how these vast changes evolved. The recruits are provided with a comparison of the "new I.A.D" and the "old I.A.D." The former Internal Affairs Bureau is described as "highly reactive," meaning the investigators possessed the ability to accept or reject reports of corruption. In essence, if complaints are not documented, then the bureau can essentially control the appearance of the department and the amount of work that would be required. Further, bureau investigators involved in misconduct can protect themselves from discovery. In comparison, the new bureau is described as being proactive and employs various investigative methods. For example, pattern analysis is used to detect organized crime. Financial and other types of criminal behaviors can be detected and investigated based on intelligence or observation. This information can be collected by interviews, documents, and surveillance. Palmiotto (2004) described pattern analysis as being effective when used to detect crimes that possess a high degree of recurrence, such as police corruption during the Knapp and Mollen eras. Based on collection of intelligence, linkages can be made to document the location of criminal activity, flow of funds or drugs, and establish members of conspiracies. Other methods used by the current Internal Affairs Bureau are sophisticated surveillance, officer integrity testing, drug testing, informants, and undercover operations. As investigative efforts are enhanced, so are the methods of storing criminal information. During the Knapp investigation, computers were not the norm and criminal information was obtained through hand collation and file drawers. Currently, the department uses automation to collect, collate, and store criminal information, which can be analyzed and used to develop crime trends or just to maintain historical data.

Structurally, the Internal Affairs Bureau presently consists of various investigative elements throughout the city that report directly to the chief of internal affairs. It is essential that such investigative activities remain confidential so that investigations are not compromised. These elements specifically investigate allegations regarding members of the Organized Crime Control Bureau (OCCB), police impersonation investigations, integrity testing of officers, surveillance efforts, excessive force investigations, and financial crimes. The OCCB is tasked with investigating organized crime within the city as well as in the department as needed. The infrastructure of this bureau consists of the narcotics division, vice enforcement division, auto crime division, gangs division, firearms suppressions division, investigative support division, and the organized crime division.

Borough Investigation Units

Aside from the Internal Affairs Bureau, recruits are also taught about the more localized investigative units. Borough investigation units are more multifaceted in their responsibilities and are not answerable to the Internal Affairs Bureau. The duties assigned to the borough investigative units now include allegations of misconduct referred by the Internal Affairs Bureau. This includes:

1. Integrity control investigations
2. Compliance with department directives through field observations
3. Various administrative duties, analysis of statistical data regarding civilian complaints, discipline, vehicle accidents, and abuse such a sick leave abuse
4. Conducting pattern analysis to identify department members for abuse
5. Conducting other investigations and inspections as deemed necessary by the borough commander

Integrity Monitoring

Of particular importance for recruit training is the class regarding the *integrity monitoring file*. This file, maintained by the integrity control officer, contains information about locations in the city that provide potential situations wherein officers may engage in acts of misconduct or corruption. Such venues are inspected by supervisors to ensure that all officers remain in compliance with department directives. Officers are directed not to frequent the following types of locations: designated off-limits locations, unlawful locations, and cooping-prone locations.

Designated Off-Limits Locations

Designated off-limits locations are legitimate business locations that have been restricted due to acts of police misconduct. It is paramount that appearances of impropriety be prevented. There is a saying that one's perception is another's reality. In this regard, even though an officer does not engage in misconduct, a perception of misconduct on the part of the public can have detrimental effects upon the officer and the department. Interestingly, not all police departments take similar actions. The department has identified such locations as restaurants offering discounts on meals or free meals for police officers; stores that offer officers free merchandise; and, of course, locations frequented by criminals (when the officers are not on official duty).

Unlawful Locations

Unlawful locations are locations where illegal activities occur. Such locations include gambling or numbers running, narcotics-prone locations, and prostitution-prone locations (and other types of vice offenses). As in the off-limits locations, officers can frequent these unlawful locations only when on duty.

Cooping-Prone Locations

Cooping-prone locations are those locations where officers tend to engage in non-police activities that interrupt patrols in an unauthorized manner. A variety of such locations can be surmised, such as spending time at home or other locations not in the officer's area of responsibility while on duty. The department provided the example of officers parking in desolate areas to sleep.

Integrity Conferrals

In light of the uncontrolled receipt of gratuities during both the Knapp and Mollen investigations, the department command instituted integrity conferrals. Since the acceptance of gratuities was perhaps the most common act of corruption, recruits receive training regarding how integrity will be maintained. Integrity conferrals were defined as "... an atmosphere of discipline, integrity, professional demeanor, and to identify problems, the commanding officer will, on a semi-basis, conduct a one-on-one conferral with each member of the command" (New York Police Department, 2015, p. 14). One program that was instituted is the *Holiday Integrity Program*. This program, which is supported by coordination between local commanders and the integrity control officers, comprises monitoring shopping conducted by officers, whether they are on or off duty. This effort is designed to prevent the receipt of gratuities being offered by local businesses. It is called the Holiday Integrity Program since these efforts occur during the months of November, December, and January. Beyond monitoring shopping, the command also inspects police parking locations to locate packages in police vehicles and the transference of packages from police vehicles to private vehicles. With an average of 33,000 police officers, these inspections can be quite a daunting task.

Supervisory Combat of Corruption

Recruits are informed that their supervisors will be responsible for monitoring their on-duty conduct. These supervisors (sergeants and lieutenants) are also available for counseling, responding to off-duty acts of misconduct, and reports of any breaches of departmental guidelines or acts of corruption.

Reporting Corruption and Misconduct

Aside from learning about corruption and its consequences, recruits are also expected to discover and report acts of corruption. This should occur whether they are on or off duty. Recall that many officers who failed to report such actions were considered to be enablers and, therefore, considered to have some complicity in corruption. Reports of suspect corruption can be made directly to the officer's supervisor. But what if the officer fears reprisals? The New York Police Department (2015, p. 16) has included the following five methods in which reports may be made:

In person: 315 Hudson Street, New York, NY
Mail: Through U.S. Mail or department mail
Phone: Internal Affairs Bureau (212) 741-8401; 1-800-PRIDE PD; or 212-CORRUPT
Fax: Internal Affairs Bureau Command Center, 212-741-8401
E-mail: IAB@NYPD.ORG

In general, allegations are received from the public via mail, phone, or in person; police officers or other personnel from the department; the Civilian Complaint Review Board; Internal Affairs investigations; written complaints to the chief of Internal Affairs, and referrals from external agencies. Previously, investigators oftentimes did not have access to information so that thorough investigations could be completed. However, recruits are now taught that the Internal Affairs Bureau maintains the needed information in its investigative computer system where raw complaints, management tools, statistical data, and tracking capabilities are available for review as needed. Officers are informed that they may submit corruption complaints anonymously, which will result in their receiving a confidential information number. However, the following caveat is provided to all officers, "Reporting corruption or other misconduct to this number meets the obligation of all members of the service to report allegations of corruption and other misconduct" (New York Police Department, 2015, p. 17). Officers are obligated to report, however, there is no way to identify the anonymous reporters. Therefore, their reports are more voluntary than the result of department obligation.

The seriousness of corruption is not overstated by the department. In addition to the aforementioned statement of obligation to report, the New York Police Department (2015) also added a forceful warning to recruits during their academy training: "All members of the service have an absolute duty to report any corruption or other misconduct or allegations of corruption or other misconduct of which they become aware" (p. 18). This now begs the question: What happens if an officer fails to make a report? Failure to report is considered to be a serious act of misconduct, and the officer may face the appropriate charges if substantiated based on inquiry. If the failure to report was based on an intent to conceal wrongful actions, criminal charges, such as obstruction of justice, conspiracy, or other crimes, may be brought with the agreement of the district attorney.

There may be times when officers receive complaints directly to themselves. In such cases, officers are required to immediately notify their supervisors to begin the process of investigating the claim. To ensure that allegations of officer misconduct are appropriately investigated, the officer *must* notify the command center of the Internal Affairs Bureau using the aforementioned telephone numbers and provide the preliminary facts of the case, full personal identification (or provide the information anonymously), and furnish details of the alleged acts of corruption or misconduct. Conversely, the officer can elect to submit a written statement.

Drug Abuse, Alcohol Abuse, and Unlawful Premises

The New York Police Department demonstrated a history of drug use, sales, and other related crimes when confronting narcotics suspects. One famous narcotics case occurred prior to the Knapp investigation (October 7, 1961–February 24, 1962), which became known as the "French Connection." This case was ultimately the focus of a book written by Robin Moore and later a film (although the film was largely inaccurate). Various narcotics violations continued to occur between Knapp and Mollen. Presently, the New York Police Department (2015) provides recruits with strict instruction regarding the use and unlawful possession of drugs. Due to the seriousness of this issue, the recruit integrity class begins with the caveat: "Once a uniformed member of this department is found to be illegally using illicit drugs – including narcotics, steroids, etc., Department policy dictates they must be terminated, with NO exceptions" (p. 22). Many industries may provide employees with rehabilitation services; however, the department does not provide this service since officers are committing crimes against laws they are sworn to uphold. Drug testing and strict management have allowed the department to boast that less than one half of 1% of officers have been found to be positive for drug use.

The drug testing program appears to be strictly enforced. This program requires that all candidates and probationary officers undergo testing three times during their entrance into the academy and full-time employment. These tests are conducted during the pre-hiring phase, during a random management visit to the academy, and at a randomly chosen time near the end of a probationary officer's initial 24 months of service. The recruits are also informed about how drug testing is administered:

Uniformed rank and file: Random selection
End of probation: All members completing their probationary 24 months
OCCB, special operations, IAB, detectives: Required, random
Promotional: Required for new supervisors
Counseling: Officers returning to duty from counseling

Upon selection for drug testing, the officer must report to the medical division unless one of the following circumstances exists: sick report, military leave, vacation, terminal leave, or bereavement leave. Officers who refuse the drug testing are to be suspended and face possible termination from the department. However, random testing requires the officer's appearance for testing and the aforementioned circumstances do not apply. Positive results of drug tests include the following repercussions: loss of income, dismissal, loss of pension benefits, and the unlikelihood of future employment with the department.

Teaching Methods

The *Police Studies Learning Outcomes* (Appendix D) are provided to recruits as a guide for their initial training in the academy. In addition to reading, reviewing, and engaging in dialogue about the consistent need for ethical behavior beyond reproach, police students engage in active learning methods. *The Police Student's Guide* provides 14 case study scenarios (Appendix E) describing allegations of misconduct and corruption. The presented offenses range from what seems a simple misuse of a department computer to police officers accused of dealing in drugs and rape. The expectation is that following the training in ethics and integrity, the police recruit will be able to recognize breaches of integrity and conduct to include those events involving off-duty officers. In some cases, the case scenario results are identified as unfounded. With completed training comes the expectation that the recruit will be able to differentiate between a bona fide infraction and those circumstances that do not support the allegation. This type of exercise inspires critical thinking for the recruit, while allowing him or her the opportunity to work through a variety of circumstances that may lead to several possible outcomes. Each case scenario provides the allegation, investigation, and result. Presenting the allegation as a scenario leads the recruit into the investigation along with rationale for the steps for examination, while then providing the recruit with possible resulting actions to take for reporting or resolution.

Acknowledgment

At the conclusion of integrity training, the recruit is required to read and sign an *Acknowledgment of Responsibilities* (NYPD, 2014). There is a list provided for specific behaviors, but there is a codicil advising that the list is understood to be not inclusive, but rather a pointed detailing of important elements, with an eye to general reinforcing of the broader ethics and integrity training provided throughout the recruit's tenure as student.

References

American Nurses Association (ANA). (2014). *Code of ethics with interpretive statements.* Retrieved from: http://www.nursingworld.org/MainMenuCategories/EthicsStandards/CodeofEthicsforNurses/Code-of-Ethics.pdf

Ethics. (2014). Retrieved from: http://www.merriam-webster.com/dictionary/ethics

Etter, G. W., & Griffin, R. (2011). In-service training for older law enforcement officers: An andragogical approach. *Policing, 34*(2), 233–245.

Mollen, M., Baer, H., Evans, H., Lankler, R., & Tyler, H. R. (1994). *Commission to investigate allegations of police corruption and the anti-corruption procedures of the police department: Commission report.* New York, NY: The City of New York.

New York City Fire Department (FDNY). (2014). *Core values of the department.* Retrieved from: http://www.nyc.gov/html/fdny/html/general/mission.shtml

New York Police Department (NYPD). (2015, July). *Police studies: Policing with integrity*. New York, NY: The City of New York.

Palmiotto, M. J. (2004). *Criminal investigation*. Lanham, MD: University Press of America.

Pollock, J. M. (2014). *Ethical dilemmas and decisions in criminal justice* (8thed.). Belmont, CA: Cengage Learning.

Walker, D. B., & Kratcoski, P. C. (1985). A cross-cultural perspective on police values and police-community relations. *Criminal Justice Review, 10*(1), 21–28.

Weiss, T. R. (2014). NYPD officers to receive city-issued Smartphones, tablets. *EWeek*. Retrieved from: http://www.eweek.com/mobile/nypd-officers-getting-city-issued-smartphones-tablets.html

6

A Tale of Two Eras

A Comparison

> ... I'm a resident and a citizen of this City. I have a vested interest that the quality of life in this City should become somewhat better, and that my wife and my children and my grandchild, together with all citizens, can point to the Police Department and truly say, "It's the finest."
>
> **Captain Daniel McGowan**

Recruit Populations

The journeys through two distinct eras of the New York Police Department, although connected by acts of misconduct and corruption, are quite different. New York City is not a stranger to inquiries, investigations, and complaints about police officers who abuse their powers and oftentimes act criminally. Averaging the officer populations of these two eras shows a rather steady officer base of 31,000 police officers. Recruit classes are quite large. In 1952 the recruit class produced 681 graduates, which eventually resulted in future suspect officers who would engage in corruption and possibly face the Knapp Commission. Recall that the Knapp Commission reported that recruits were frequently pressured into joining the ranks of the corrupt. Between 1992 and 1995, a time when corrupt officers would face the Mollen Commission, 10,125 officers were added to the department. These recruits were incrementally added as follows: 2,104 recruits in 1992; 2,942 recruits in 1993; 2,600 recruits in 1994; and 2,479 recruits in 1995 (Weiss, 2012). In comparison, in 2014, 884 police recruits graduated, bringing the officer population to 34,423 (Sutherland, Gonen, & Golding, 2014). Beginning in 2015, 891 recruits took their oaths and began the 6-month journey into law enforcement (City of New York, 2014). It is interesting to note that the hire rate of officers in New York City decreased. Considering the earlier years and their recruitment numbers, the hire rate may tend to explain the corruption problems found by both commissions. Both commissions reported that recruitment efforts were lacking. Since 1994, no large-scale corruption investigations have occurred. This is not to say that corruption has not existed within the department. Corruption on a smaller scale has occurred. For example, New York County District Attorney Cyrus R. Vance (former Knapp Commission commissioner) published a press release dated January 7, 2014, regarding a large conspiracy in which 106 defendants were indicted for Social Security disability fraud. Of this number, 80 were retirees from the New York Police Department and the New York City Fire Department (Vance, 2014). The conspirators, guilty themselves, convinced other Social Security Disability Insurance recipients to lie about their psychiatric condition to collect disability payments to which they were not entitled. Police Commissioner William Bratton related this crime to the victims of September 11, 2001. Commission Bratton (as cited in Vance, 2014) offered the following statement in part:

> The retired members of the NYPD indicted in this case have disgraced all first responders who perished during the search and rescue efforts on September 11, 2001, and those who subsequently died from 9/11 related illness, by exploiting their involvements that tragic day for personal gain.

Corruption Patterns Then and Later

While perusing the emphasis of each commission, it can be seen that the variety of corruptive activities decreased from 1972 to 1994. The Mollen Commission concentrated mainly on more violent crimes and narcotics. In 1972, narcotics violations and corruption were a small segment of the larger number of corruption patterns. The majority of the patterns indicated that, by and large, corrupt officers were more interested in making money through contacts with citizens who desired special treatments for their businesses. Narcotics was a *dirty business* and produced fear of prosecution and incarceration. The patterns documented by Mollen (5) were only 39% of the patterns documented in 1972 (13). Of the five patterns in Mollen, three addressed narcotics (pattern 1: Cops committing theft; pattern 2: Cops protecting and assisting narcotics traffickers; pattern 3: Cops as drug dealers and users—distributing and using drugs; and pattern 4: perjury and falsifying documents). Pattern 4, even though it did not specifically mention narcotics, applied as well, since officers perjured themselves during most, if not all, acts of corruption.

The fifth pattern of corruption, brutality, was important enough to be included as a separate problem for the department. The Knapp Commission did not discuss brutality to any great extent. In fact, it is rarely mentioned in its report. However, in Mollen, brutality was linked between corruption and the police culture itself. This is a great departure from the previous corruptive acts in 1972 that centered on money. In short, compared to 1972, the officers in 1994 became more aggressive criminals by committing more violent crimes. The question to ask is: why did corruption patterns change so drastically? The Mollen Commission attempted to explain the difference between 1972 and 1994. In their estimation, "The corruption of a generation ago was primarily characterized by a mutually beneficial accommodation between cop and criminal. Criminals offered bribes in return for immunity from arrests and cops accepted them" (Mollen, Baer, Evans, Lankler, & Tyler, 1994, p. 17). In other words, the Knapp era was a matter of money with some more violent crimes thrown in. The briberies were considered both systemic and hierarchal in nature, almost to the point of extreme complication since protection within the department was extended to everyone. Money always played an important part of the corruption scheme. However, the corruption patterns changed to more lucrative means as pointed out by Mollen et al. (1994):

> In contrast, today's corruption is primarily characterized by serious criminal activity. Officers in numerous narcotics-infested precincts throughout the City routinely stormed drug locations and stole whatever drugs, money or other property they could find; they stopped drug dealers and their vehicles and stole from them openly; and they sometimes used violence to carry out these activities (p. 17).

In addition to bribery or extortion, the patterns added robbery, theft, aggravated assault, murder, and kidnapping. It appeared that, for some reason, police officers desired money and opted to take any means necessary to gain it.

Command Attitudes

One item that did not change between 1972 and 1994 was the attitude conveyed by the administration and command officers. In both instances, the administration desired to conceal any behaviors that would tarnish the department's image before the community. Currently, the New York Police Department is experiencing a tarnished image resulting from officers conducting their duties. This recent issue has come about due to alleged police brutality (similar to that found in the 1994 commission investigation) that initially occurred in Ferguson, MO, and spread countrywide. The images of the department in 1972 and 1994 were also held by the community at large regardless of the patterns found. Similarly, in 2014 factions of the community have held the opinion that *all* police officers violate their powers and authority. The primary difference between 1994 and 2014 is that the officers were, for the most part, acting within their authority and not through corruption.

The administration during the Knapp investigation placed the blame of corruption on two types of officers: the legendary *rogue* officer who acted alone and the impressionable recruit who indulged in corruption based on pressures from peers and veteran officers. The rogue theory began the *rotten apple* theory explaining the cause of corruption. The administration continued to ignore the primary reason for corruption, that being the image of the department and damage to the infrastructure to include the loss of rank and pay. During the Mollen Commission, the rogue officer was believed to be a myth since there were too many organized groups participating in drug operations. The administration had no option but to recognize this situation and could not pass the blame onto individuals acting in spurious manners. Here, too, the administration went to great lengths to ignore the issues of corruption. There were no claims that only lone officers were engaging in corruption. A different method was used to deny systemic corruption. The deeper the infection, the more encouraged the commanders and top managers felt to deny the problem by permitting controls to wane to the wayside and to refuse necessary resources to find corruption.

Departmental Investigations of Corruption

Issues facing both commissions were similar in nature. Basically, the department was failing to adequately conduct investigations for a variety of reasons. In Knapp, the Inspection Services Bureau (ISB) was formed to organize the various units that were charged with finding misconduct and maintaining integrity and efficiency. These units were the Internal Affairs, Inspection Division, Intelligence Division, and the Public Morals Administrative Division. However, the department could not claim that they were doing a stellar job. The initial failure of this bureau was due to the lack of authority and resources; this was a collapse of the intent to investigate corruption. Not only was this plan a failure in itself, but also the official recognition of the ISB never occurred and the bureau had to operate without standing. Overall the department suffered from a lack of manpower, poor investigative techniques, and a lack of coordination during investigation assignments. Along with poor record keeping, which included disorganization and missing documents, the poor attitudes of investigative and management personnel showed they were concerned about conducting investigations that might tend to disprove the rotten apple theory. With the assistance of such personnel, the department was being supported in its lie that the department was managed and free of systemic corruption.

The comparison of the department's investigative mechanisms between 1972 and 1994 produced a vastly different situation, albeit very similar in intent. It appeared that the 1972 department failed due to attitudes and poor performance. In 1994 the department continued the effort to hide corruption but in more definite terms. While the 1972 department neglected to carry out important tasks (for example, not supporting the ISB), the 1994 department did not bother to carry out investigative responsibilities. The Internal Affairs Division (IAD) abandoned its charter to investigate corruption and the department hierarchy conveyed the notion that no one cared. With the amount of serious corruption and misconduct in the department, it makes sense that the IAD would choose not to divulge corruption depending on the gains realized by the investigators. In order to conceal this, the IAD focused on small and insignificant acts. The Field Internal Affairs Units (FIAUs) were to support the IAD; however, these units were permitted to erode into uselessness because of the lack of support and management from the IAD. Not only did the IAD not support the FIAUs, but also the department commanders failed to support them as well. Clearly, but also the issues should have come to the attention of the administration; however, due to administrative attitudes, little was done about it until the commission arrived.

Two Cultures

It appears that the culture of police corruption varied between the Knapp Commission investigation and the Mollen Commission investigation. One similarity remained: the general attitudes of the command structure and of the police officers themselves. As stated earlier, not all officers were corrupt and many conducted themselves according to their mandates and training. This does not mean that these officers had no hand in the corruption. In many instances, these officers were enablers of those who indulged. They did not gain monetary rewards or property through participation. The only gain they could realize was through their tacit approval of corruption by their inactions and their refusal to combat corruption. In short, no matter who the officer was, the department was almost entirely corrupt. This refusal to bring corruption to light was the result of possible threats or personal injury. The most celebrated example of this was Officer Frank Serpico. As widely known, Officer Serpico resented and refused participation in corruption. The first incident was an envelope containing $300, which was handed to Officer Serpico for participation he never had but as encouragement to join the group. Not wanting to be involved in corruption, Officer Serpico brought this to the attention of authority who explained to him: "He could go to the Commissioner of Investigation who would send him before a grand jury, after which he might well wind up 'in the East River'; or he could forget about the incident" (Knapp et al., 1972, p. 197).

Two other aspects of the culture of corruption were similar between the investigations. The first aspect was the sense of loyalty among the corrupt officers. This loyalty helps hide acts of misconduct. Being loyal to any group sets a standard of conduct that the group demands. Getting into this group is easy, but attempting to leave is usually very difficult. Wright, Dinsmore, and Kellaris (2013) found that those who gain affiliation with others in a group are rewarded through positive feelings and attitudes. Perhaps this means that there is always strength in numbers and the loss of positive feelings and attitudes is undesirable. Once a member seeks to leave a group, tensions rise and distrust begins. Wright et al. (2013) stated, "A transgression by an in-group member against the in-group may seem more loathsome because it carries two offenses: the transgression itself is compounded by the sin of disloyalty" (p. 206). Recall the story of Officer Serpico and his abandonment from the group of detectives who were collecting money from victim citizens. Once these officers joined these groups, unswerving loyalty was expected and nothing was more important, not even stopping serious systemic corruption that might corrupt the entire department. The second aspect is the attitudes displayed by the officers. Some officers have gone as far as using the department radios to send code messages to alert their partners against discovery or arrest. As mentioned above, the normally non-offending officers decided to protect other officers and cover up their crimes. These two aspects held true for both commission investigations.

Both investigative eras maintained the theory of the *code of silence.* This was the strict unwritten rule that officers do not rat on officers as shown in this testimony by Bernard Cawley:

Question: Were you ever afraid that one your fellow officers might turn you in?

Answer: Never.

Question: Why not?

Answer: Because it was the Blue Wall of Silence. Cops don't tell on cops. And if they did tell on them, just say if a cop decided to tell on me, his career's ruined. He's going to be labeled as a rat. So if he has fifteen more years to go on the job, he's going to be miserable because it follows you wherever you go. And he could be in a precinct, he's going to have nobody to work with. And chances are if it comes down to it they're going to let him get hurt (Mollen et al., 1994, p. 53).

The Mollen Commission discussed the erosion of one's values and pride. This is also discussed in Chapter 5 during the review of the recruit training guide. The Knapp Commission did not exactly discuss this; however, since the behaviors they investigated were very similar, it can be assumed that officers did forfeit their values and pride during the acts of misconduct. The Mollen Commission, as can be expected, related this to the narcotics in the city. Recall that the narcotics trade in the city involved theft of drugs and money, illegal vehicle stops and searches, bribery, and the possession and use of confiscated narcotics. How can officers, who are frequently exposed to this life style, prevent the forfeiture of their values about narcotics especially in light of the pressures placed upon them by other corrupt officers? Part of the responsibility also belongs to the department administration for not pressuring officers not to indulge in acts of misconduct. This poor command attitude was almost identical during each investigative era.

Pride is also shared by the commission investigations. Pride can be seen in two ways: through dignity and self-respect through good work and one's pride through personal achievements, however corrupt they may be. Officers who indulge in misconduct by being incompetent, untrustworthy, and undisciplined should not be working alongside officers who are not corruption prone. The Mollen Commission found that officers can develop a perverted pride of themselves, which then results in them acting out while in uniform.

Cynicism and morality were also shared by both commissions. New police officers can maintain their morality by resisting the corruption of their values and pride. Cynicism can be present in most officers who practice acts of misconduct. For example, the city and department maintain their view about what the police department should be. However, this vision may not be realistic on a daily basis. Those officers who become cynical oftentimes are drawn toward corruption. For example, if the detectives can collect money from businesses, why not the patrolmen? If officers receive large payoffs from drug dealers, then why log the evidence into the evidence room? Each commission investigation found that these problems existed in the department on a large scale.

Beyond Knapp and Mollen

Both the Knapp and Mollen Commissions revealed a plethora of corruption and misconduct that evolved from rather insignificant gratuities to murder. A look into the future beyond Mollen, as expected, revealed that corruption and misconduct continued. The question is to what degree did these acts continue? The department produced a report covering the dates of January 1 through December 31, 2013. The report provided a breakdown of complaints regarding officer behaviors. It was noted that the sources of these complaints were chronic callers already known by the department. The allegations were varied with larceny being the most generally recognized crime (although only one complaint was received). Of the 26 categories of complaints, nine were found to be significantly higher in number. The complaints were abuse of authority (13), criminal association/criminal activity (16), disagrees with department policy or actions (15), disputed arrest or summons (40), FADO (representing actions such as excessive force, abuse of authority, discourtesy, and offensive language) (34), failure to take police action (51), others non-NYPD (25), others miscellaneous (66), and unable to determine the exact nature of the complaint (43). In total, this log contained 375 complaints. The importance of this complaint log is that there is no specific mention of narcotics, bribery, extortion, robbery, or assault, which were prevalent in the Knapp and Mollen investigations. However, this does not mean that those types of crimes did not occur (Armstrong, Chin, Landis, & Zirin, 2014).

This report also clearly delineates the process in which complaints are currently received and processed. Referred to as *principles*, the department listed four important aspects of this process: all complaints are to be investigated regardless of the complainant (*comprehensive*); the complaint process should be easily afforded to complainants (*accessible*); all investigations are to be of high quality work (*fair and thorough*); and complainants are to be kept appraised of the status of the investigation (*transparency*). The results of these investigations could be listed in the following categories: *substantiated*, *partially substantiated*, *unsubstantiated*, *exonerated*, and *unfounded*.

At the time of this report, the department maintained 102 pending cases of the most serious allegations. The behaviors with allegations were *bribery* (1), *criminal association* (17), *excessive force* (3), *false statements* (4), *firearms* (1), *missing property* (20), *narcotics* (2), *sex offenses* (3), and *other* (5). Other allegations consist of a wide variety of less serious issues. Interestingly, the receipt of gratuities is in this category. Overall, this report documented pending complaints, closed complaints, sources of information, complaint statuses, and substantiated allegations. It was found that criminal association maintained a higher number of allegations. Also of interest was that of the closed cases, the sources of complaints were rather equal between civilian complainants (29) and department personnel (28). This is a vast contrast as compared to the Knapp and Mollen findings. Recall that the department opted to deny the existence of corruption as a systemic problem. Currently, the department emulates the recommendations of the Mollen Commission and new innovations to combat corruption.

References

Armstrong, M. F., Chin, K. H., Landis D. E., & Zirin J. D. (2014). *Commission to combat police corruption: Sixteenth annual report of the commission, October 2014.* Retrieved from: http://www.nyc.gov/html/ccpc/assets/downloads/pdf/Sixteen-Annual.pdf

City of New York. (2014). *New class of 891 police academy recruits sworn into service.* Retrieved from: http://www.nypdnews.com/2015/01/new-class-of-891-police-academy.html

Knapp, W., Monserrat, J., Sprizzo, J. E., Thomas, F. A., & Vance, C. R. (1972). *Commission to investigate allegations of police corruption and the city's anti-corruption procedures: Commission report.* New York, NY: Braziller.

Mollen, M., Baer, H., Evans, H., Lankler, R., & Tyler, H. R. (1994). *Commission to investigate allegations of police corruption and the anti-corruption procedures of the police department: Commission report.* New York, NY: The City of New York.

Sutherland, A., Gonen, Y., & Golding, B. (2014, December 29). Traitor de Blasio booed at police academy graduation. *New York Post.* Retrieved from: http://nypost.com/2014/12/29/traitor-de-blasio-booed-at-police-academy-graduation/

Vance, C. R. (2014). *106 defendants, including 80 NYPD and FDNY retirees, indicted in social security disability fraud costing federal taxpayers hundreds of millions* [Press release]. Retrieved from: http://manhattanda.org/press-release/da-vance-106-defendants-including-80-nypd-and-fdny-retirees-indicted-social-security-d

Weiss, M. (2012). *NYPD to lose thousands of cops to retirement over next few years.* Retrieved from: http://www.dnainfo.com/new-york/20120919/new-york-city/nypd-could-lose-thousands-of-cops-retirement-over-next-few-years

Wright, S. A., Dinsmore, J. B., & Kellaris, J. J. (2013). How group loyalties shape ethical judgment and punishment preferences. *Psychology and Marketing, 303*(3), 203–210. doi: 10.1002/mar.20598

Appendix A: Legal Aspects of Corruption

Appendix A lists portions of the law of New York State regarding offenses committed during acts of corruption (New York Laws, n.d).

Article 105: Conspiracy

105.00 Conspiracy in the *sixth degree* (class B misdemeanor): A person is guilty of conspiracy in the sixth degree when, with intent that conduct constituting a crime be performed, he agrees with one or more persons to engage in or cause the performance of such conduct.

105.05 Conspiracy in the *fifth degree* (class A misdemeanor): A person is guilty of conspiracy in the fifth degree when, with intent that conduct constituting:

1. A felony be performed, he agrees with one or more persons to engage in or cause the performance of such conduct.
2. A crime be performed, he, being over 18 years of age, agrees with one or more persons under 16 years of age to engage in or cause the performance of such conduct.

105.10 Conspiracy in the *fourth degree* (class E felony): A person is guilty of conspiracy in the fourth degree when, with intent that conduct constituting:

1. A class B or class C felony be performed, he or she agrees with one or more persons to engage in or cause the performance of such conduct.
2. A crime be performed, he or she, being over 18 years of age, agrees with one or more persons under 16 years of age to engage in or cause the performance of such conduct.
3. The felony of money laundering in the third degree as defined in section 470.10 of this chapter, be performed, he or she agrees with one or more persons to engage in or cause the performance of such conduct.

105.13 Conspiracy in the *third degree* (class D felony): A person is guilty of conspiracy in the third degree when, with intent that conduct constituting a class B or class C felony be performed, he, being over 18 years of age, agrees with one or more persons under 16 years of age to engage in or cause the performance of such conduct.

105.15 Conspiracy in the *second degree* (class B felony): A person is guilty of conspiracy in the second degree when, with intent that conduct constituting a class A felony be performed, he agrees with one or more persons to engage in or cause the performance of such conduct.

105.17 Conspiracy in the *first degree* (class A-1 felony): A person is guilty of conspiracy in the first degree when, with intent that conduct constituting a class A felony be performed, he, being over 18 years of age, agrees with one or more persons under 16 years of age to engage in or cause the performance of such conduct.

Article 135: Kidnapping, Coercion, and Related Crimes

135.20 Kidnapping in the *second degree* (class B felony): A person is guilty of kidnapping in the second degree when he abducts another person.

135.25 Kidnapping in the *first degree* (class A-1 felony): A person is guilty of kidnapping in the first degree when he abducts another person and when

1. His intent is to compel a third person to pay or deliver money or property as ransom, or to engage in other particular conduct, or to refrain from engaging in particular conduct.
2. He restrains a person abducted for a period of more than 12 hours with intent to
   a. Inflict physical injury or violent or abuse him sexually
   b. Accomplish or advance the commission of a felony
   c. Terrorize him or a third person
   d. Interfere with the performance of a governmental or political function
3. A person abducted dies during the abduction or before he is able to return or be returned to safety. Such death shall be presumed, in a case where such person was less than 16 years old or an incompetent person at the time of the abduction, from evidence that his parents, guardians, or other lawful custodians did not see or hear from him following the termination of the abduction and prior to trial and received no reliable information during such period persuasively indicating that he was alive. In all other cases, such death shall be presumed from evidence that a person whom the person abducted would have been extremely likely to visit or communicate with during the specified period were he alive and free to do so did not see or hear from him during such period and received no reliable information during such period persuasively indicating that he was alive.

Article 155: Larceny

155.05 Larceny, defined: A person steals property and commits larceny when, with intent to deprive another of property or to appropriate the same to himself or to a third person, he wrongfully takes, obtains, or withholds such property from an owner thereof.

155.25 Petit larceny (class A misdemeanor). A person is guilty of petit larceny when he steals property.

155.30 Grand larceny in the *fourth degree* (class E felony). A person is guilty of grand larceny in fourth degree when he steals property and when the value of the property exceeds $1,000.

155.35 Grand larceny in the *third degree* (class D felony). A person is guilty of larceny in the third degree when he or she steals property and when the value of the property exceeds $3,000.

155.40 Grand larceny in the *second degree* (class C felony). A person is guilty of grand larceny in second degree when he steals property and when

1. The value of the property exceeds $50,000.
2. The property, regardless of its nature and value, is obtained by extortion committed by instilling in the victim fear that the actor or another person will (a) cause physical injury to some person in the future, or (b) cause damage to property, or (c) use or abuse his position as a public servant by engaging in conduct within or related to his official duties, or by failing or refusing to perform an official duty, in such a manner as to affect some person adversely.

155.42 Grand larceny in the *first degree* (class B felony). A person is guilty of larceny in the first degree when he steals property and when the value of the property exceeds $1,000,000.

Article 200: Bribery Including Public Servants and Related Offenses

200.00 Bribery in the *third degree* (class D felony). A person is guilty of bribery in the third degree when he confers, or offers or agrees to confer, any benefit upon a public servant upon an agreement or understanding that such public servant's vote, opinion, judgment, action, decision, or exercise of discretion as a public servant will thereby be influenced.

200.03 Bribery in the *second degree* (class C felony). A person is guilty of bribery in the second degree when he confers, or offers, or agrees to confer, any benefit valued in excess of $10,000 upon a public servant upon an agreement or understanding that such public servant's vote, opinion, judgment, action, decision, or exercise of discretion as a public servant will thereby be influenced.

200.04 Bribery in the *first degree* (class B felony). A person is guilty of bribery in the first degree when he confers, or offers or agrees to confer, any benefit upon a public servant upon an agreement or understanding that such public servant's vote, opinion, judgment, action, decision, or exercise of discretion as a public servant will thereby be influenced in the investigation, arrest, detention, prosecution, or incarceration of any person for the commission or alleged commission of a class A felony defined in Article 220 of the penal law or an attempt to commit any such class A felony.

200.10 Bribe receiving in the *third degree* (class D felony). A public servant is guilty of bribe receiving in the third degree when he solicits, accepts, or agrees to accept any benefit from another person upon an agreement or an understanding that his vote, opinion, judgment, action, decision, or exercise of discretion as a public servant will thereby be influenced.

200.11 Bribe receiving in the *second degree* (class C felony). A public servant is guilty of bribe receiving in the second degree when he solicits, accepts or agrees to accept any benefit valued in excess of $10,000 from another person upon an agreement or an understanding that his vote, opinion, judgment, action, decision, or exercise of discretion as a public servant will thereby be influenced.

200.12 Bribe receiving in the *first degree* (class B felony). A public servant is guilty of bribery in the first degree when he confers, or offers, or agrees to accept, any benefit from another person upon an agreement or understanding that such public servant's vote, opinion, judgment, action, decision, or exercise of discretion as a public servant will thereby be influenced in the investigation, arrest, detention, prosecution, or incarceration of any person for the commission or alleged commission of a class A felony defined in Article 220 of the penal law or an attempt to commit any such class A felony.

Article 220: Narcotics

220.00 Controlled Substances Offenses.

220.03 Criminal Possession of a controlled substance in the *seventh degree* (class A misdemeanor).

A person is guilty of criminal possession of a controlled substance in the seventh degree when he or she knowingly and unlawfully possesses a controlled substance; provided, however, that it shall not be a violation of this section when a person possesses a residual amount of a controlled substance and that residual amount is in or on a hypodermic syringe or hypodermic needle obtained and possessed pursuant to section 3300.81 of the public health law; not shall it be a violation of this section when a person's unlawful possession of a controlled substance is discovered as a result of seeking immediate health care as defined paragraph (b) of subdivision 3 of Section 220.78 of the penal law, for either another person or him or herself because such person is experiencing a drug or alcohol overdose or life threatening medical emergency as defined in paragraph (a) of subdivision 3 or Section 220.78 of the penal law.

220.06 Criminal Possession of a controlled substance in the *fifth degree* (class D felony). A person is guilty of criminal possession of a controlled substance in the fifth degree when he knowingly and unlawfully possesses a controlled substance with the intent to sell it.

220.09 Criminal Possession of a controlled substance in the *fourth degree* (class C felony). A person is guilty of criminal possession of a controlled substance in the fifth degree when he knowingly and unlawfully possesses a narcotic with the intent to sell it.

220.16 Criminal Possession of a controlled substance in the *third degree* (class B felony). A person is guilty of criminal possession of a controlled substance in the third degree when he knowingly and unlawfully possesses a narcotic with the intent to sell it.

Appendix B: Charge Data of Police Officers 1968–1972

Bronx County Charge Data: 1968–1972

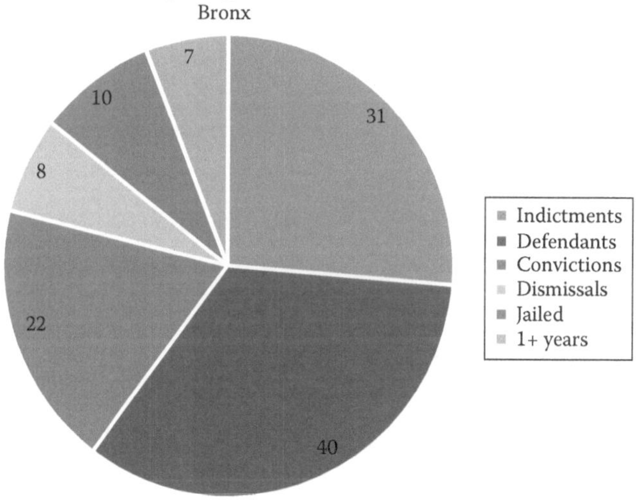

New York County Charge Data: 1968–1972
Manhattan

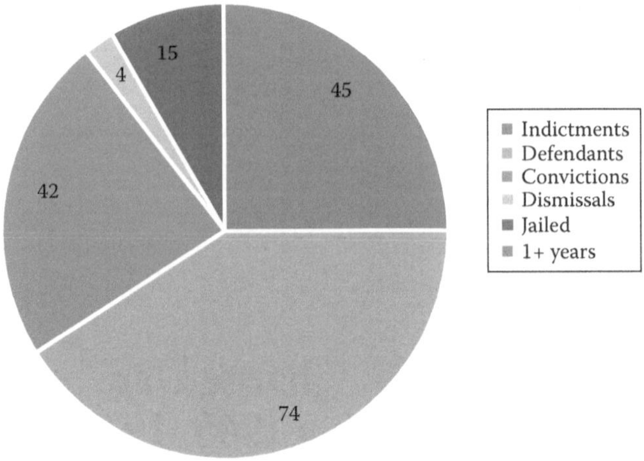

Queens County Charge Data: 1968–1972
Queens

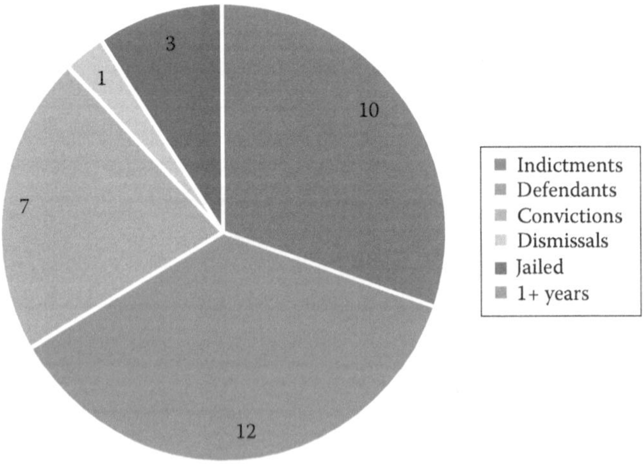

Kings County Charge Data: 1968–1972
Brooklyn

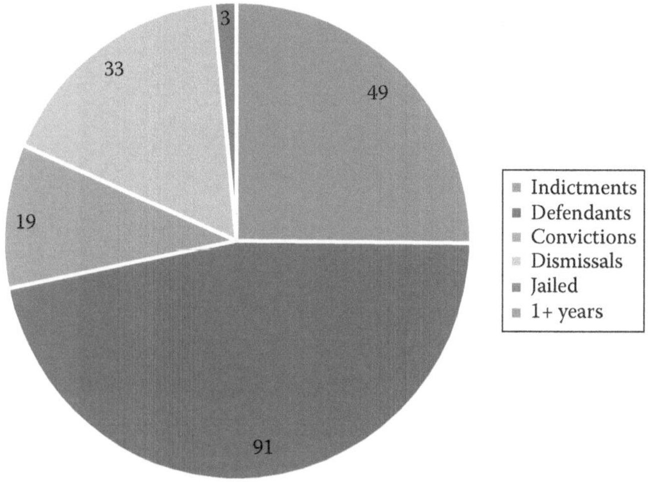

Richmond County Charge Data: 1968–1972
Staten Island

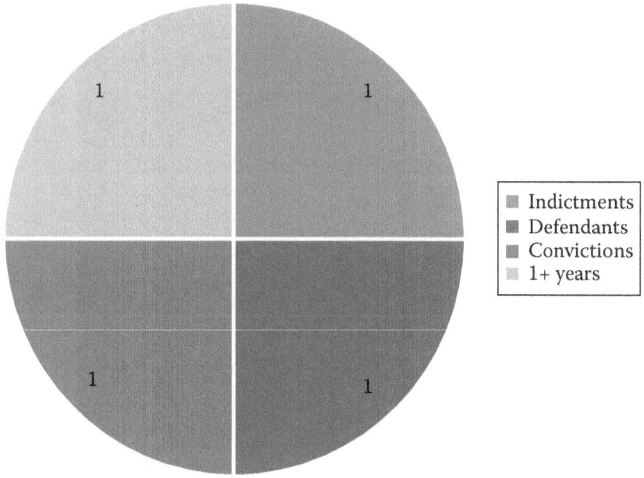

Appendix C: Police Code of Ethics

A police officer is both a citizen and a law enforcement officer who, on behalf of his fellow citizens, prevents crime, preserves the public peace, protects persons and property, and apprehends offenders.

It is the tradition of the police profession to be helpful to all beyond the call of duty.

A police officer is a servant of the law. Honesty in thought and deed should characterize a police officer's official and private life.

A police officer must be impartial and fair to all people, whatever their social position, race, creed, age, ethnicity, gender, or sexual orientation.

A police officer must be incorruptible to be worthy of his chosen profession. Honest police officers must not tolerate an officer who would engage in corruption or other misconduct.

All police officers have an absolute duty to report any corruption or other misconduct of which they become aware.

A police officer should have compassionate respect for the dignity of the individual and behave to all with courtesy, self-control, human understanding, and tolerance.

A police officer must never use more force than necessary to accomplish a legitimate purpose nor may he ever subject anybody to any form of cruel, inhuman, or degrading treatment.

A police officer should strive continually to increase his professional skills. In so doing, the officer should seek to gain ever greater insight into society and human nature.

A police officer must execute the laws and regulations of his jurisdiction and obey orders pursuant to such laws and regulations.

Matters of official police department business coming to the attention of a police officer should be kept confidential, unless the performance of his official duties requires otherwise.

A police officer's conduct as a citizen should be exemplary.

Source: New York Police Department (NYPD) (Chapter 3, p. 5).

Appendix D: Police Studies Learning Outcomes

1. Discuss Department values and Police Code of Ethics and explain how they are associated with police integrity.
2. Discuss the history of corruption in the NYPD.
3. Identify the mission and function of the Internal Affairs Bureau and other investigative units.
4. List the ways allegations/complaints come to the I.A.B. and the ways in which a member of the service can report corruption.
5. Explain the Department policy concerning drug abuse, alcohol abuse, and patronizing unlawful premises.
6. Describe the NYPD policy on drug testing.
7. Describe the 14 categories utilized in tracking trends of corruption.
8. Explain the dispositions given to cases investigated by Internal Affairs.

9. Identify proper actions regarding domestic violence and arrests of an MOS.
10. Review and discuss the 14 case studies of allegations of other misconduct or corruption.
11. Discuss the contents of the "Acknowledgment of Responsibilities."

Source: New York Police Department (NYPD) (Chapter 3, p. 5).

Appendix E: Case Studies of Allegations of Misconduct/Corruption

1. Misuse of Department computer
2. Allegation of money taken from a prisoner and not returned
3. Dispute between two police officers
4. Dole Test—Random
5. Dole Test—Targeted
6. Police officers visiting a drug location
7. Police officer allegedly kidnapped a child
8. Off-duty police officer arrested for DWI
9. Police officer allegedly took $10.00 from complainant's vehicle
10. Police officer arrested for leaving the scene of a vehicular collision
11. Police officers engaging in auto insurance frauds
12. Police officer arrested for forcibly raping a female
13. Housing Bureau police officer arrested or robbing drug dealers
14. Police officer deals pharmaceutical drugs; is arrested, and commits suicide

Source: New York Police Department (NYPD) (Chapter 3, p. 29).

Index